To
Joe Dutton!

Best of luck
in the deer :)
woods

Jim Burnell
1/11/97

To Heck With Deer Hunting

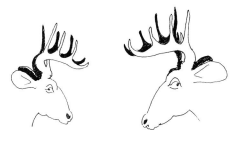

By
Jim Zumbo

All Photos by The Author

Illustrations by Boots Reynolds

ISBN: 0-9624025-3-2

Published by:

Jim Zumbo
Wapiti Valley Publishing Company
Box 2390
Cody, WY 82414

Publishing Consultant:

**STONEYDALE PRESS
PUBLISHING CO.**

205 Main Street, Drawer B, Stevensville, MT 59870 • (406) 777-2729

TABLE OF CONTENTS

INTRODUCTION

If you've hunted deer much, or maybe just a little, you've no doubt been frustrated with the way some of your hunts have worked out. One thing is for sure — hunting is unpredictable. All sorts of things can foul up your plans; in fact, more hunters go home without a deer than with one.

This book describes a number of my deer hunts around the country in which I tried to focus on the more humorous aspects of the outings. About half the book is about whitetails; the other half about muleys and blacktails.

In addition, I tell the circumstances of each hunt, including the little things that made it a success or failure. By doing so, I've tried to inject as much information as possible. We learn by our mistakes. I've made lots of mistakes, but I've always tried to figure out how to improve my hunting strategies. The ones that worked are passed on to you in the book. The ones that didn't work are passed on, too.

The intent of *TO HECK WITH DEER HUNTING* is to make you smile. I believe humor has its place in hunting. To that end, I've drawn upon some of my funniest moments in the deer woods, like the time I was told I shot the camp mascot to the time me and my pals spent a night in jail.

I hope you'll laugh a little and learn a lot. If so, this book is a success.

Jim Zumbo
Cody, Wyoming

A TEENAGER LEARNS ABOUT WHITETAILS

Whitetail deer are often called the smartest big game animals in North America. Having been outfoxed and outmaneuvered by whitetails over the years, I have to agree. A smart old buck can evaporate like smoke, and he'll play games on you that will make you think he can reason.

I learned about whitetails early on, but it took plenty of years before I figured them out to the point where I could hunt them with some degree of success.

As near as I can recall, the first whitetail I ever saw was near Beacon, New York, a town just across the Hudson River from Newburgh, N,Y., where I was born and raised. My mother's uncle owned a fireworks factory, and stored his powder in sheds located in a large woodlot adjacent to a forest.

I was visiting the fireworks plant with my Dad and uncles when a huge buck bounced out of a weedy gully and disappeared into the woods. At least, to my 8-year-old eyes, the buck was huge. Maybe he was a modest 6-pointer or whatever — all I saw was a handsome animal with antlers on its head as it bounded away. I'll never forget the big white tail swishing about to and fro.

My uncle Phil, who was the hunter of the family, made a comment about hunting the buck when deer season arrived. I remember wishing that I'd like to hunt it too, but at that point in time I was just getting acquainted with my first BB gun.

I accompanied my uncles, grandfather, and my Dad on hunts as I grew older. My Dad was only marginally interested in hunting, but he was an avid fisherman. Most of our early hunts were for cottontails. My grandfather had beagle hounds; my memory bank can still conjure the sounds of those little dogs as they chased rabbits through patches of brush.

I bought a deer tag as soon as I was old enough to hunt, but all I saw on my trips were white flags waving goodbye. It seemed I saw only the rear ends of deer rather than their foreparts.

Most of my hunting was on the Black Rock Forest, a 9,000 acre wooded area owned by Harvard University. Hunting rights on the forest were reserved for members of the Black Rock Fish and Game Club, which had 1,000 members and a long waiting list to join. Since my Dad and uncles were members as long as I can remember, I was allowed to join as soon as I was old enough. Sons of members had first rights.

Through the years, I had a close companion who was more like a brother than a friend. Lou Gizzarelli and I met in Boy Scouts, and were inseparable. We hunted and fished together constantly, and never missed opening day of anything, whether it was for trout, bass, pheasants, grouse, squirrels, or deer.

No matter how hard I tried for deer, I couldn't spot a buck in a shootable position. As I recall it now, I was doing everything wrong, but I didn't know it at the time. I didn't know how to slip through the woods quietly, I didn't watch the wind, or penetrate the woods enough. Lou and I hunted hard, but it seemed we always had bad luck. We had no trouble finding fresh gut piles, however, which were silent reminders of what might have happened had we been at that spot a couple hours or a day or two earlier.

After I graduated from high school, I went to a two-year forestry college in northern New York. My life-long ambition was to be a game warden, but those jobs were tough to get. Forestry careers were a bit easier to come by.

Paul Smith's College is about 50 miles south of the Canadian border, and nestles in a rugged chunk of the Adirondack Mountains. I was bound and determined to get my first buck while attending school. The area was known for big bucks, but it was very remote. Swamps and heavily timbered forests were the domain of the heavy-bodied bucks that inhabited the mountains.

I lived in a dormitory set back in the woods three miles from the highway. Called White Pine Camp, it was actually an old retreat owned by some wealthy folks, and subsequently sold to the college. There were about 10 buildings in all, including two dormitories, mess hall, and several outbuildings. The camp was adjacent to Osgood Pond, a lake that contained some superb northern pike. At the headwaters of the lake, an expansive swamp ran almost up into Canada. Locals called it Dead Man's swamp, because a number of people had become lost in it and never found their way out. It was said that if you walked north, you could go 40 miles before hitting a road. Maybe some of that information was exaggerated; maybe not. To us teen-age foresters, however, Dead Man's Swamp was a piece of cake. We were proud kids, and, as freshmen forestry students, we figured we knew everything there was to know about the woods.

It was tough to find time to hunt. Classes and studies consumed most of our time, but during my first fall as a freshman I had every intention of hunting Dead Man's Swamp. A couple classmates wanted to go along, so on a Saturday morning we rowed an old boat up the lake in the dark, using a flashlight to guide us along the shoreline. None of us had been that far before, but we were enthusiastic over the prospects of shooting one or more of the very big bucks that inhabited the swamp.

It was just breaking light when we eased the boat up to the bank. Soon we were in the big woods, a timbered area that held sugar maple, yellow birch, and big white pine trees. A bit of exploring took us into lowlands, where a vast swamp crept into every pocket and valley. Sphagnum moss carpeted the swamp — a spongy growth that quivered and sunk a little as you stepped on it. Stunted spruce trees grew in the swamp; nothing else could tolerate the stagnant water.

Our hunting mode was simply to still hunt slowly, keeping in sight of each other now and then. For some reason our little party remained intact — no one drifted off by himself.

By mid-morning we were deep in the swamp, and our hunting had produced nothing. Sign was sparse, though big bucks were certainly present. If the truth were known, we wouldn't have recognized sign if it hit us over the head.

We decided to head back to the boat and try an area closer to the dormitories. Locals told us that it held some big bucks. They also told us to avoid Dead Man's Swamp because it was tough to hunt and only a skilled woodsmen would take a buck out of it. I suppose that's the reason we went there. To three 18-year-olds, nothing was impossible, especially when those teenagers were proud foresters who knew all about such things as swamps, big bucks, and deer sign.

When we made the decision to go to the boat, we immediately launched into a discussion as to the direction of the lake. Each of us figured it was a different way than the other person.

To resolve the dilemma we agreed to try one direction and follow it a half mile. If we didn't see the lake, which really was a narrow channel where we left the boat, we'd try another direction.

Two hours later, after trying three directions, the fact that we were a mite turned around began to sink in. More discussion followed, which ended in a show of fear, concern, and uncertainty. No one was willing to admit we were lost. We had no compass, and each of us had no firm conviction as to the way out.

Finally, one of my pals reached the breaking point. He showed signs of panic, and his usual calm disposition was replaced by a fiery temperament. He started running aimlessly, and began to cry. He was sure he'd never see his mother and father again, and didn't want to die a horrible death in Dead Man's Swamp. His hysteria seemed to strengthen me and my other pal. We grabbed him and calmed him down, telling him that we had plenty of matches and that someone would certainly come looking for us when we didn't show up. To be truthful, I wasn't so sure I'd ever see my Mom and Dad again, either. The woods and swamp, which were friendly when we were studying them in forestry classes, were now sinister entities to be feared.

After another hour of walking in the swamp, we were sure we'd be added to the list of people who had disappeared forever.

Suddenly we heard two quick shots close by. We immediately took off running toward the direction of the shots, and came upon two hunters sitting on a small knoll. They were locals, and had shot at and missed a black bear that we'd evidently pushed toward them.

Seeing real humans instantly changed our disposition. Gone were the horrible fears; the nightmare of being lost. We nonchalantly walked up to the hunters and made small talk.

My forestry classmates and I gather around a huge swamp buck taken by a local hunter in New York's Adirondack mountains. It was the biggest whitetail we'd ever seen, with a dressed weight of 240 pounds.

"By the way", one of us said, "what's the quickest way to Osgood Pond? We wanted to try another place before dark and don't have much time left."

What a lie. However, it was a way to save face, and our enormous teen-age egos would remain intact.

The hunters pointed out the easiest direction to the boat. We thanked them, and headed off. A half hour later we found the lake and the boat, and we never mentioned the incident for the duration of our college years. It was a secret that we kept between us.

I learned a valuable lesson on that hunt, one I never forgot. Unless there are landmarks, or the area is easy to become oriented in, I carry a compass, and many times I'll use a map as well. As long as I live, I'll never forget that morning of terror in Dead Man's Swamp.

A couple weeks later, I tried still hunting through a horrible hemlock-spruce-pine thicket that was wrapped in vines and saplings. The spot I hunted was 100 yards from the dirt road between our dormitory and the highway, but it might as well have been 100 miles away. The jungle I tried to negotiate was a world in itself. I'd seen the tracks of a very big buck where it had crossed the road in the snow, and decided to give it a go. Other hunters had seen a big buck in that area for years; in fact they called him Old Joe.

I was squeezing through a horizontal slot between two snowy logs when I heard a muffled explosion right under my nose. For a split second I caught a glimpse of giant antlers as the huge buck disappeared instantly in the thicket. If it wasn't Old Joe, it was his brother. Though I hunted for him the rest of the season, I never saw him again. I found his tracks, but I never got close. I was too inexperienced, and I'm not sure I could have successfully tracked Old Joe today, after more than 35 years of hunting whitetails.

Old Joe was partially responsible for my writing career. I was so impressed with the wise old buck that I wrote an article about him and submitted it to the college newspaper. The editors liked it and printed it, and I tried writing a few more articles. They too were published. I didn't know it then, but I was building toward a vastly different career other than forestry. About 20 years later I'd give up my forestry job and write full time for *OUTDOOR LIFE*.

One evening the following fall, we were sitting around in our dormitory, talking about hunting whitetails. Most of my forestry classmates were avid hunters, and in fact, only 2 or 3 of the 35 of us at White Pine Camp didn't hunt.

It was about an hour after dark when someone asked about Dave. He'd gone deer hunting that day, and wasn't back yet. No one was really worried. Dave was born at the edge of the Adirondacks, and was one of the best woodsmen in the entire college. He was known for striking out early in the morning, hiking over several big mountains, and returning after dark, usually with a big buck lying in the woods, field dressed and needing plenty of manpower to retrieve it from its remote location.

Another hour passed, and someone looked out at the thermometer. It was 25 degrees below zero, and snow was piled two feet deep, but we still weren't worried. The bitter cold and deep snow was normal for northern New York in late November, and Dave knew how to handle himself in the arctic environment.

When yet another hour passed, we started getting worried. Skilled or not, Dave should have been in long ago. We knew he couldn't be lost — Dave was too good in the woods, but we were afraid he'd gotten hurt. He wouldn't last long in the cold if he couldn't get a fire going.

We called the police and divided up into groups. We were going to organize a search, though it would be tough going in the dark. It was one of those pitch black nights with heavy clouds obscuring the stars and moon. The snow reflected just enough light so we'd be able to see a bit, but we'd rely on flashlights and lanterns.

Before leaving, we spread out a map and tried to figure where Dave might be; then we decided where we'd start to look. At best, all we could do was to fire shots in the air and hope he'd answer and fire back. Trying to find his tracks and follow wouldn't do much good, because we weren't sure where he'd gone, and we might make a confusing maze in the snow for an extensive morning search.

We were just about to head out when we heard a loud thump at the door. It was Dave, covered from the top of his head to the bottom of his boots with ice and snow. He was lying on the porch, and had managed to crawl and drag himself the last quarter mile to the dormitory. The thump we heard was his fist as he managed to draw enough strength to punch at the door.

We knew Dave was in big trouble. He was almost delirious, and was suffering from hypothermia. His legs and boots were completely encased in ice an inch thick. There was hardly any movement possible at his knees; he had to walk as if on stilts.

Quickly we removed most of his clothes, and positioned him near a roaring fire. It was impossible to remove his frozen pants and boots without cutting them off, so we slowly immersed Dave's legs in a bathtub filled with luke warm water. As soon as we got his frozen clothes off, we got some hot beverage into him, wrapped him in warm clothes, and took him to the emergency room at the hospital 20 miles away.

The doctors took one look at Dave and got to work immediately. I don't know what they did, or what they thought, but someone mentioned the possibility of gangrene and amputation, and I immediately felt nauseous, as did the rest of my classmates. We went back to the dormitory, mighty upset and worried.

To our great relief, we learned the next day that Dave would probably be okay, though he had some badly frostbitten toes. He continued to improve, and was soon released from the hospital.

Dave told us what had happened. He'd killed a big buck at the edge of a swamp just before dark. He field dressed it, marked its location with a ribbon tied to a tree, and headed out. While crossing a beaver swamp, the ice gave way and Dave plunged in to water up to his waist. He was able to get out quickly, but the bitter cold air immediately froze his clothes. As he slogged through deep snow in the night, the cold and moisture penetrated deeper, until his legs were literally encased in ice.

I went back for Dave's buck four days after he'd killed it with my classmates, Andy and Ted. We found the buck under 18 inches of fresh snow, and never would have found it at all if it wasn't for the ribbon Dave had tied in the birch tree above the deer.

As a 19-year old forester, I figured I knew everything there was to know about the woods. I was wrong; I'm still learning.

While dragging the frozen carcass back to the dormitory, I lost a glove in the deep snow. I couldn't find it, and continued on with a bare hand. As a result, I ended up with two frostbitten fingers that still occasionally hurt when my hand gets cold.

After he recovered, Dave never said to heck with deer hunting, as a lot of other people might have in that situation. The rest of us didn't either, but we surely learned to respect bitterly cold temperatures.

Those northern New York whitetails taught us plenty of extra lessons, outside of our studies in forestry school. Those lessons weren't in the books, either.

I might be smiling in this photo, but I'm really half-frozen. High country deer hunting has its perils. (Photo courtesy Ralph Stuart.)

THE BUCKS STARTED HERE

Being a successful deer hunter depends on a number of factors. Luck is one of them, but there are more important circumstances. The state and area you hunt plays a valuable role. If you're hunting public lands in California or New York, for example, your odds will be terrible. Your chances of getting a deer will be about 10 or 15 percent. In Wyoming, where I live, it will be as high as 75 percent. Obviously, the place you hunt means everything.

I was raised in southern New York about 60 miles from New York City, and the area surrounding my home town wasn't exactly a great spot to hunt deer. To be sure, there were plenty of whitetails around, but there were enormous numbers of hunters, too. As I explain elsewhere in this book, my teenage hunting years drew blanks. I didn't get a deer while I was in high school, and I was also unsuccessful while attending forestry college in New York's rugged Adirondack mountains.

I never really had a good mentor who was wise to the ways of whitetails. Most of my family members loved to hunt and fish, but whitetail deer hunting simply involved standing in a spot and hoping that someone would push a buck your way.

I guess I was a pretty lucky kid. All my life I wanted to work outdoors professionally, hopefully as a game warden, and I eventually went on to college and became a forester. A couple of my close buddies wanted to work outdoors too, but they succumbed to city life and took on other occupations.

I was raised in a city where houses jammed up tightly against each other, but I had a devout attraction to the outdoors. I remember lying on the sidewalk, feeding bread crumbs to ants, and watching the ants hustle each tiny crumb into their hole. I gave names to spiders that lived in the hedge around the house, feeding them daily a healthy diet of flies, ants, and, when the spiders were big enough, crickets and grasshoppers.

I read hunting and fishing magazines constantly, and marveled at the big deer pictured on the pages. Early on I wanted to go west, to see with my own eyes the magnificent Rockies and the animals that lived within them. I secretly wished that I was born on a big western spread, growing up as a cowboy and doing all the things that cowboys do.

After receiving a two-year Associate Degree in Forestry from Paul Smith's College in the Adirondacks, I made a decision that would have a profound effect on the rest of my life. The two-year degree wasn't much good in a forestry career, at least the kind of career I wanted, so I decided to go on for my Bachelor's degree. It seemed that several of the Paul Smith's graduates had gone to Utah State University for their Bachelor's, and since I had a friend who went there, he strongly urged that I go out.

For a kid who had hardly been much more than 200 miles from home, and who had done very little traveling, the idea of going out to Utah was mind-boggling. I might as well have been going to Saudi Arabia or Australia. Utah and the Rocky Mountains were faraway places that held a great deal of mystique and, for me, was the land of the great unknown.

My first trip to Utah was via a bus. I was 19 years old when I departed from my hometown, and I remember being bombarded with all sorts of feelings when the bus pulled away from the depot. Mom was in tears, of course, as we waved goodbye, and Dad tried his best to hold back his emotions as well. After the bus had gone a few miles out of town, however, the sadness of leaving home eased into excitement. A big adventure lay ahead as my life began charting its course toward manhood.

This vintage car was our hunting rig while I was a student at Utah State University. It didn't get us very far in the woods, but it served its purpose.

The bus rolled west, stopping every hour or two to take on passengers, refuel, stop to change drivers or to allow us to eat a meal. It was an uncomfortable trip, and I found it almost impossible to relax in the confounded seats, especially when I wanted to sleep.

I don't remember how long we were on the road, maybe 40 or 50 hours, when I looked out the window just as the sun was rising in the east. The incredibly beautiful alpenglow cast an orange-golden sheen on the landscape outside the bus, and I became abruptly awake when I saw, for the first time, real sagebrush, buttes and mesas rising from the desert floor.

"Good Lord," I thought to myself, "I'm in the WEST. I'M REALLY HERE!"

I couldn't get enough of the scenario outside the speeding bus. I lowered myself in the seat to look through the window at a lower vantage point, because the upper area was tinted. I wanted to see the west in all its true splendor.

Suddenly I saw animals grazing on the prairie. I recognized them instantly, even though I'd never seen them before.

"Antelope!," I said aloud. "Those are really antelope!" I was so excited I was beside myself, and couldn't contain my feelings.

The passenger next to me was a big, fat, man, and he was fast asleep, just like everyone else on the bus. When I shouted out the word, "antelope," he opened one eye, grunted, and quickly resumed sleeping.

It was just as well, because I was a proud teenager, and I wouldn't have wanted anyone, even strangers, to see the tears of joy sliding down my face. It was a time for privacy, a time to try to grasp the enormity of what was going on inside my brain. To put it simply, I was an exquisitely happy young man. The whole world was right, at that moment in time.

Some hours later, we finally arrived in Logan, Utah, my destination point. Logan is the home of Utah State University, and is a lovely, clean town nestled next to a series of high, steep mountains. This was the Wasatch Range, part of the Rockies, and I was awed at their sight. I conjured images of all the animals that lived there, animals that didn't live in New York. Mule deer, elk, mountain lions, and all sorts of new creatures would soon be objects of my curiosity. I couldn't wait to see

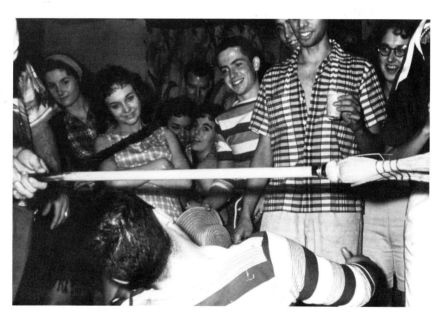

If you're old enough to remember the Limbo fad, you'll recognize this scene. Hunting time was often shared with social events such as these.

my first muley.

But first of all, I needed a place to live. I had made arrangements to live in a men's dorm, but I wasn't totally comfortable with that option. I'd have a strange roommate, and I would have preferred to pick my own, rather than to have the college do it. To complicate matters, the dorm room would be available to me only for a couple weeks, because I hadn't reserved it early enough. I'd have to find another place to live.

As soon as I got off the bus at the station, I walked across the street to an old hotel. I dragged a huge foot locker loaded with all my belongings, because the dorm room wasn't open until morning. I had a reservation at the hotel for one night.

The people who I saw and talked to seemed right friendly. I didn't know what to expect, because I was told that the majority of Utahns are Mormons. I'd never met a Mormon before; all I'd heard was that they spend a lot of time in church, and don't smoke or drink. As far as I could tell, after a few hours of being around people who I assumed were Mormons, they appeared to be pretty fine folks. They had two ears, five fingers on each hand, and all the other correct features required of humans. I liked their easy going attitude, too. A couple things bothered me, though. At that point in time, I smoked plenty of cigarettes — unfiltered Lucky Strikes that were fashionable among macho guys my age, at least back in New York. Alcohol was also no stranger. As a kid I'd helped my Dad, Grandpa, and uncles make wine in the basement. By the time I reached drinking age, which was 18 in New York, I had alcohol under control, and knew how to drink socially without becoming a raging drunk as many of my buddies did.

After an uneasy night in the hotel, I went for a walk through town. I hadn't gone three blocks when I saw an off-campus fraternity house that had a prominent sign outside that read, "boarders wanted". It was an old cobblestone house with Greek fraternity symbols over the porch. Something about the house seemed warm and friendly.

I figured I had nothing to lose, so I walked up, screwed up my courage, and knocked on the door. To my surprise, the guy who answered the door had a beer in his hand and a smile on his face. He invited me in, and I was introduced to three other men who were playing poker and drinking beer. When I introduced myself and told them that I had just gotten in from New York and was relieved to know that there were some people around who drank beer, I was amazed to learn that they were all from New York, and all students at the university. A beer was immediately offered to me, which I accepted.

My next action, within the next three minutes, was to agree to live in the house, and within a half hour my huge foot locker was transported from the house to my new bedroom, thanks to my new roommates and a beat-up pickup truck. I canceled the dorm room, which was fine with the college because it was only a temporary situation anyway.

As it turned out, the next couple of years in the fraternity house could be easily compared to the situations presented in the movie

Fraternity life took its toll on my hunting endeavors, but the boys and I always found time to head for the forests.

"Animal House," starring John Belushi. I could write an entire book alone on the shenanigans we were involved in, but this is a book on deer hunting and I'll ignore that wacky period of my life. Suffice to say I never broke any laws, ended up in jail, or hurt anyone. That's about all I care to say on the matter. Somehow I managed to keep my grades up, though a number of ladies, parties, and saloons were constant deterrents. I guess that in this book of confessions I can say that I hocked my Winchester Model 94 .30/.30 carbine so I could take a pretty lass to a prom. It was obvious that my priorities were badly reversed in those days, but back then I didn't think quite as clearly as I might have — a common problem with lots of young college men, then and now.

The first two deer seasons were failures. As a college student, I had little time for anything except studying and quite a bit of partying. I hunted a close-by national forest with pals, but we didn't do any good. The forest was mobbed with hunters, just as it is today. We hunted a few hours on weekends, but the crowds of people made for tough hunting.

I was amazed at the heavy hunting pressure. When I lived in the east, I assumed the west was truly the wide open spaces with lots of room to roam. A lot of it indeed was, and is today, but not public land in Utah. It's an absolute circus.

On the bright side, I was delighted with the lack of posted signs. Federal land was new to me. I could literally hike for weeks on national forest and BLM land and never see a sign. It was a pleasure to know that all those millions of acres were free and open to public hunting.

My first serious deer season occurred when I met a lady and she invited me to hunt with her relatives in a part of Utah I'd never visited. I was ready for a serious deer hunt. Here I was, almost 22 years old, and still hadn't gotten a deer.

Camp was a huge tent pitched on the edge of a small juniper forest. Vast expanses of sagebrush blanketed the land, but I really didn't have a total picture of the area because I'd arrived in the night.

On opening morning my companion and I were driven to the hunt area by our mentor. He parked the ancient Ford pickup somewhere in the sea of sagebrush and instructed me and my friend to walk half-way down a canyon slope and sit until he showed up at mid-morning.

We carefully picked our way down through the rocks, and settled into a position that looked good in our flashlight beam. It was pitch black; shooting light was still a long way off.

Watching the birth of a new morning is always a magical experience, unless you're sitting still and it's real cold out. It was, in fact, real cold, and a lot of the magic was transferred into shivering and waiting for the confounded sun to appear. Until it did, however, I waited impatiently for light. As slowly as possible, distant shapes began to take a crisp form, and I was able to identify objects around me. Soon it was light enough for me to realize that the entire canyon below me was covered with low sage about knee high.

"There are no trees here," I said to my companion. "Why are we

A little rodeo occurred when our horse refused to pack my buck.

hunting where there are no trees?"

My friend wasn't sure. She was no help.

The sun was just lighting the ridgetops when I looked down and saw a dandy buck sauntering along a trail in the middle of the canyon bottom. He was but a mere 100 yards away, and, for the first time in my life, I had a good shot at a living, breathing deer.

My rifle was a .303 British Enfield that I'd borrowed from a classmate. I longed for the friendly carbine that I'd hocked, but that rifle was history.

I swung with the buck, keeping him nestled in the open sights, but I was the victim of buck fever. I was shaking so badly that I was unwilling to pull the trigger. The buck was moving along at a fair pace; soon he'd be out of sight around the bend.

My friend, who indicated she wanted me to shoot the first deer, was evidently irritated at my hesitation and hissed that if I didn't shoot, she would.

The trance was broken and I was galvanized into action. Immediately the sights settled down and I squeezed the trigger. The buck was hit, and instead of running a few yards forward and out of sight, he lunged up onto the slope opposite us. Two more shots anchored him, and he was mine. Jack O'Connor would have been proud.

Our mentor showed up and when he took a look at the buck lying in the sage, claimed that it was one of the heaviest bodied bucks he'd ever seen in a lifetime of hunting. I had no idea how big the buck should have or might have been. If he had been as big as a bull elk I wouldn't have known any better.

A few hours later, we had the buck tethered to a horse, but not until after a short rodeo. I learned something about packing game on horses that day: Murphy's Law is ALWAYS close by.

Back at the farm, the buck field dressed 232 pounds on accurate grain scales. I was a mighty happy hunter, even though the deer didn't have a huge rack. It was a very old buck, having four points on one side and five on the other. The rack was very heavy, but the tines were short, probably due to his old age.

I was ready to say to heck with hunting in treeless country that opening morning, but the buck made me a believer. My first buck taught me something right off the bat, and though I've taken about 60 muleys in eight states as I write this, I've been learning ever since. I'm still learning.

I approach a nice eight-point whitetail buck I took at West Point.

WHITETAILS AT WEST POINT

If anyone was to ask you what West Point was all about, you'd immediately think of one of our most famous military academies, and of course, lots of legendary generals. Grant, Custer, Eisenhower, Patton, Westmoreland, Swartzkopf — these and many others were products of the Long Gray Line.

What you DON'T associate West Point with is hunting and fishing. The fact is, the installation has an outstanding wildlife program, which is a surprise to almost everyone I've ever talked to about it.

I worked at West Point from 1966 to 1974 as Post Forester, Game Warden, Wildlife Biologist — you name it — if it was in regard to the woods and water located on the 16,000 acre military reservation, I was involved in it.

I applied for the job after having worked as a forester for the state of Utah for two years. The West Point job offered a great career opportunity, and a nice raise. Besides, I felt the Utah forestry position wasn't much of a challenge, and I wasn't sure the government agency had much of a future. Since I had plenty of in-laws in Utah, I'd be motivated to visit there annually, and hunt muleys and elk.

Among other things, my job at West Point included managing the whitetail deer herd that was bustling at the seams. Deer were so plentiful you could easily see 50 or 100 in a day, but that huge population took its toll in the health of the herd and the woodlands. Too many deer

West Point cadets pose with my dog, Pepper, after we got back from a bird hunting trip to another military installation.

translated to small, undernourished animals, and a considerable amount of overgrazing in the forest.

A hunting program was initiated to thin deer numbers, but it wasn't very effective because does were illegal quarry. Each year, hunters took an average of 50 to 60 bucks from the forest. The overall population kept spiralling upward, but I wasn't able to initiate a doe season. That was the responsibility of the New York State Department of Environmental Conservation.

The weight of the average buck was about 100 pounds. A big buck was 130 pounds. The biggest buck I ever weighed during my eight years at West Point was a 163-pound brute, killed by a cadet. All weights were field-dressed.

As part of my duties, I maintained a hunting headquarters office. I had to carefully record physical data for each buck killed. All deer taken on the installation had to be weighed on accurate scales, aged, and their antlers had to be measured.

Aging was done by measuring tooth wear. In order to learn that little chore, I had to annually attend a class at the NY DEC's central office in Albany. Me and several game wardens had to take a one-day course, in which we looked at hundreds of deer jaws and measured them. At the end of the day we were tested by having to estimate the ages of 10 sets of jaws. The instructor liked to have a little fun with us by tossing in a weird jaw, such as one from a deer that ate a lot of soft, succulent food, and never wore down its teeth normally. Or a jaw from a deer from Georgia or South Carolina that lived in a sandy area, adding much more wear to the teeth than usual.

The hunting program was set up so that no more than five hunters could hunt a unit at a time. That was done on a first-come first-served basis, with the exception of opening day and the following day, which was done in a lottery draw. The first-come first-served part was handled by having a sign-up sheet at my office. Hunters would drive up early in the morning to sign up, and because you couldn't make reservations or sign prior to midnight of the day you wanted to hunt, you can imagine the big jam-up to get the best units. Of course, some hunting areas were much better than others, and competition was fierce. I was at my office by 5 a.m. every morning, and by then there was usually a long line of hunters waiting their turn at the sign-up list.

The lottery selection was accomplished at a mandatory orientation meeting that I conducted. If you wanted to hunt deer, you had to attend the meeting, pure and simple. The agenda included post hunting regulations, safety procedures, off-limit areas, and the draw for the first two days.

An interesting phenomenon developed when I commenced the lottery procedure. During my eight years at West Point, only one general was an avid outdoorsman. There are three generals at the Academy -- the Superintendent, Dean of Students, and Commandant of Cadets. The general who loved to hunt always had first choice in the lottery draw. Not because he was lucky and drew Number 1 out of the box, but because I handed him the Number 1 slip before the hat was passed. This bit of propriety was highly encouraged by my boss, a full-bird Colonel, who was in charge of all natural resources at the installation. This general (whose name escapes me) loved to hunt big game, small game, birds, and he was crazy about fishing.

Before I stocked trout in the streams and lakes each spring, and before hunting season, the general called me into his office. After he invited me to settle into a very comfortable chair, and offered a fine cigar, he got down to business. Where, he asked, were the biggest bucks hanging out? I usually suggested he try Area 14, which seemed to produce the biggest bucks with the heaviest racks. The general was a good hunter, and always took a decent whitetail, regardless of the area he hunted. He was a good guy, too. When I stocked trout, he showed up in his fatigues, and helped me carry heavy pails laden with trout from the truck to the stream. His aides fussed and worried when he was precariously balanced on a rock with an eighty pound milk bucket in his hands, but he paid them no mind. Of course, by helping me stock trout, the general learned which pools received the fish. All he wanted, though, was a couple hours of relaxation the following weekend. He'd catch a few trout and release them, and be happy as a clam.

Running the deer hunting program made me the envy of the local citizenry who weren't allowed to hunt on the military reservation. The only eligible hunters were cadets, military personnel assigned directly to West Point, and civilians who resided on the post. Other than those three categories, there was one single exception — me. When I initially accepted the job, I was told that one of the perks would be permission to hunt. Any hunting I did would be during off-duty time, of course, and I'd use my own vehicle and gear.

I was born and raised in Newburgh, New York, just a dozen miles up the Hudson River from West Point. My pals and I were well aware of the fabulous hunting there, but I never dreamed I'd be able to hunt the Academy grounds.

I never made a big deal of my hunting experiences. I kept it low key, because I knew it could be a pretty sore subject. To my knowledge, my friends never seriously held it against me, but I was subject to lots of teasing. Throughout my tenure, I tried to open the post up to hunting by civilians who didn't live on the installation, but I was never successful (Some time after I left, the powers-to-be allowed off-post civilians to hunt does and fawns).

A number of amusing incidents occurred while I worked at West Point. A memorable one involved an old school buddy who was picked up by Military Police for trespassing. I should mention that trespassing on the military reservation was considered to be a justifiable violation by many local hunters. Most of West Point's woodland acreage was added to the Academy during the Second World War by condemning adjacent

Bucks like these were few and far between at West Point, but every now and then a good one would show up.

private land. Many of those landowners were unhappy with the land grab, and hunted in spite of rules. As it was, many locals knew the country far better than any of the military personnel who, at best, spent three years there before being transferred.

When my pal was picked up by MP's, I got a call on my radio. The police wanted me to transport the violator to the Provost Marshal's office. It was tough to stifle a hearty laugh when I pulled up to take my buddy in.

He got in my jeep, and I started laughing pretty good. My pal wasn't too amused, and didn't see any humor in the situation. I told him that the worst thing they'd do was to give him a stern warning and let him go. I really shouldn't have laughed, because he was upset, but I couldn't help myself. My friend received a bit of a lecture and was released.

Another time, while driving a backwoods road, I saw a hunter running through the trees. Obviously he was somewhere he shouldn't have been, or thought he was, and was trying to hide from me. As I drove closer, he dove for a sparse patch of brush which was the only cover around. It was a hilarious situation because he was dressed in hunter orange from head to toe, even gloves. He virtually glowed as he lay on the ground. I drove by chuckling, and didn't bother to tell him that he wasn't on the reservation at all. It was a quarter mile away.

On yet another occasion, my predecessor was driving through the woods in his jeep, and was attacked and captured by a bunch of cadets involved in war maneuvers. Despite George's claims of innocence, they didn't believe he was the post forester and locked him up in the compound. He was released later when someone finally identified him.

There were some pretty good reasons why off-post civilians weren't allowed to hunt on the post, or at least on some parts of it. A good share of the woodlands are used for artillery, mortar, and machine gun practice. Live rounds and duds on those ranges posed dangerous hazards.

On several occasions, while fighting forest fires or going about my duties in the woodlands, I practically stepped on live 105 mm artillery rounds, shells that are as big as your forearm and thicker than your wrist. Those were always sobering experiences.

Once, while helping a cadet drag a deer out of the woods, we dragged it directly over a live 105 shell. It was hidden under a fresh blanket of snow, and was a couple miles from the artillery range. I spotted it when the deer carcass brushed snow away from it.

Fighting forest fires was one of my major duties in the summer. Many times fires were caused by incendiary shells being used at the various ranges. We let many of those fires burn, but when they advanced beyond certain boundaries, we put them out.

It was interesting to watch the reaction of deer during the fires. Most of the time they'd carry on their feeding activities in the thick smoke, not the least bothered by it. Even more interesting was their disinterest in gunfire at the ranges. Many times I'd watch deer behind or alongside the ranges. They had no inclination to move away.

Someone once reported to me that a deer was killed by one of the range officers during practice. As the story was told, he couldn't help seeing the buck out there behind the targets, and simply shot the deer. It was deer season, but hunting in and around the range areas was off-limits because of safety reasons.

The man allegedly gutted the deer, legally tagged it, and took it home. I turned the information over to the MP's, since I didn't have authority to do a search. Besides, I wasn't terribly bothered by the incident. The accused had a legal hunting license, hunting season was open, and he shot the deer during legal hunting hours. It was a military problem, so I let the military handle it. I recall the MP's recovered the deer, but there wasn't much of a fine, if any.

For the most part, military personnel and cadets were a joy to work with. They were well-behaved, they followed the rules, and were well-disciplined. I had few problems with them as outdoorsmen.

One day a sergeant came in to my office, obviously upset. As it turned out, he'd shot a buck, but there was an unseen doe standing next to it. The bullet went through the buck and continued into the doe, killing both deer. The man was almost distraught, and wanted me to follow through with all the prescribed legal procedures. In cases like that, I turned the information over to the state game warden. When I did, he investigated, took the doe carcass, let the man keep the buck, and did not issue a ticket.

The cadets were a pleasure to work with. A small percentage of the Corps of Cadets were avid hunters, some so avid that they would rather hunt deer than go to the traditional Army-Navy football game which always took place during the deer season. That's dedication.

Occasionally a cadet would shoot a deer but run out of time to get it out of the woods before dark. They had very strict curfews and lived according to rigid schedules. Many times they'd stop by the office and inform me as to their plans of retrieving the deer. Generally they'd make arrangements for an officer to do it the next day if they had classes. Or I'd do it myself and leave the deer at my office for them to pick up the next day.

Now and then I'd be asked to accompany a group of cadets on a hunting trip. This was an R & R trip, and was usually made to a nearby installation for quail, grouse, or woodcock. I never quite got over the fact that I was being paid to take cadets bird hunting.

Another activity I participated in, and one that wasn't much fun, was to remove deer struck by vehicles from highways. I did this day and night, weekends and holidays. Most of the time it happened late at night when I was home a dozen miles away. Unfortunately, the MP's would not touch a carcass, and called me immediately. Sometimes I'd have to leave home 2 or 3 o'clock in the morning only to move a carcass three feet off the pavement.

In all my years at West Point, a few memorable and unpleasant situations arose that I had to deal with. One involved a bunch of deer that were working over the nursery that was located next to a steeply timbered hillside. Deer would come down at night and help themselves to the ornamental trees that were being raised for officer's homes. My boss, who was in charge of the nursery, told me to get a permit from the state and begin controlling the herd by shooting the deer at night. He tried every other way to stop the deer, from using repellents to electric fences. Nothing worked.

There was no way I wanted to shoot the deer, not only because I didn't want to execute them, but because I knew word would get out and I'd be ridiculed by civilians who had no permission to hunt on the post. I was pretty sensitive to those opinions. As I already mentioned, I grew up in the local area.

I had no choice but to start a deer control program, at least if I wanted to keep my job. It took some time, but I finally got the required state permit to shoot the deer. I had not, however, informed the Provost Marshal at West Point of my intentions. My boss was supposed to do that.

When I arrived late one evening with my .30/06, I told the MP at the gate that there'd be some gunfire from up in the direction of the nursery. He was aghast, and asked if I had gotten permission from the Provost Marshal. I said I hadn't but my boss probably had, and the MP told me to wait until he checked.

I began to see the solution to the dilemma, because I just knew my boss hadn't bothered to make the necessary arrangements. I was right. The Provost Marshal said, in no uncertain terms, that there'd be no shooting of firearms within the post proper, which is where the nursery was. He never allowed permission, either, even though my boss tried. I think the PM was upset because he hadn't been contacted at the outset, and wasn't about to ever give his approval.

There was another memorable incident, this one almost ending in tragedy. A doe was struck and killed by a vehicle along one of the post roads, and her newborn fawn stood over her carcass after the accident. Someone brought the fawn to my office, and I immediately bought a baby bottle and started feeding milk to the fawn. The state game warden for the area, a legendary and colorful character, gave me permission to do whatever I wanted with the deer, since none of the local zoos wanted any more fawns.

I took the deer home, and it was a big hit in the neighborhood. I called it Bucky, an appropriate name because of its sex. The local kids loved Bucky, but when it started raiding petunias and other plants and shrubs, it soon wore out its welcome. I gave it to an acquaintance who built a one-acre enclosure for Bucky.

All went well for several years. His first set of antlers were forked-horns, the next year he was a six-pointer, and the following year he'd developed a fine eight-point rack. During the peak of the rut, when he was carrying eight points, he suddenly and viciously attacked a neighbor who was cleaning the deer's pen. The neighbor was just as well acquainted with Bucky as the owner; something triggered a violent outburst in the deer. The buck had the man pinned to the ground with its antlers, and the owner ran out with a gun after hearing the screams. Moments later, Bucky had met his end. The man had no choice but to shoot it — so violent was the encounter. The game warden, who is now deceased, was worried that the newspapers would pick up the story. The man who owned Bucky didn't have a proper permit — the warden knew about the deer but wasn't much of a paperwork fan, so he let it ride.

The West Point job was a superb experience, but after eight years I transferred to the West, working with muleys, elk, and other western species. I kept up with whitetails by hunting them in the West as well as annual hunts to other states. As I write this, about 20 years after I left West Point, and having had a good deal of experience hunting big game around the continent and abroad, I still rate the mature whitetail buck as the wariest of all our species.

They're so smart that plenty of folks say to heck with deer hunting after a miserable and unsuccessful season. However, most of those folks change their minds and go back the next year. It's tough to stay out of the whitetail woods — once whitetail hunting gets in your blood, it tends to stay there.

MY BEST WHITETAIL EVER

Whitetails had been so elusive during my teen-age years that I'd almost given up on ever getting one. After finishing a two-year forestry college in northern New York, I went west to Utah and remained there for six years. Whitetails were not forgotten when I hunted muleys and guided mule deer hunters in Utah, and I couldn't wait to get back in whitetail country. Most western states have whitetails, but Utah isn't one of them. As an always-broke college student, and a struggling young forester with a minuscule paycheck, I couldn't afford to hunt out of state.

In 1966, when I decided to take a job offer at West Point as forester for the U.S. Military Academy, one of the primary motivations for the move was to hunt whitetails. Of course, my career was also a major consideration, but I couldn't wait to finally tag my first whitetail buck.

My chance came when I was invited to hunt with Paul Jeheber, a fellow employee at West Point. Paul was an avid hunter as well as an avid bird-watcher and photographer. He lived in a house nestled in the forests of the Hudson Valley, and knew the surrounding woods as well as anyone.

The hunt with Paul was during the fall of my first year at West Point. We headed out to a rocky ridgetop that Paul had hunted over the years. Our party included Steve Macica, who worked as a forestry technician for me at West Point, and the late Gene LeBleu, a dear friend who taught me much about hunting whitetails, ruffed grouse, and trapping beaver.

Paul's strategy was to put on a drive. He and Gene would walk along the ridge, while Steve and I would take positions as standers. I quickly learned that this was to be a precise operation.

"See that rock there?" Paul said as he pointed to a huge rock. "Sit on it and watch that trail to the right of that red oak tree." Again he pointed, and identified a trail that led off the ridge into a dense hemlock forest. "Your buck will be 68 yards away when he shows up. Give us 25 minutes to make the drive. If we flush deer, I'll caw like a crow. Get ready if you hear me"

I dutifully sat on the rock while Paul took Steve to another position around the bend. The rock was oddly shaped, resembling a rocking chair. For that reason, it was fondly dubbed, "rocking chair rock."

At that point in time, I'd taken several muleys in Utah and figured I was a pretty experienced deer hunter. After having studied forestry for five years in college, worked as a forester, and hunted since I was 12, I considered myself a right good woodsman. While sitting on Rocking Chair Rock, however, I was shaking like one of the quaking aspens in a pretty Utah draw. The prospect of getting a shot at a live whitetail was totally unnerving.

About 20 minutes after Paul and Gene left, I heard a crow cawing. The sound was off-key enough so I knew it was Paul rather than a real crow. With trembling hands I propped my .30/06 Winchester against a tree and got ready. This was it.

The deer didn't make much noise before I saw it. I heard a light swishing sound in the forest, and then the buck showed up, trotting along the trail. As soon as I saw antlers, I centered him in my scope. Suddenly the buck stopped and looked around.

Buck fever hit me hard as I tried to hold the rifle steady. It was all I could do to concentrate and try to calm myself down. I had to hurry, because the deer wouldn't stand there very long.

I mustered up all the nerves I could, took a deep breath, and squeezed the trigger. The buck went down instantly.

I couldn't believe it. I finally got a whitetail, and I was as excited as a hunter can be, even though my deer wasn't exactly a candidate for the record book. He was a forked-horn, but I was plenty proud of him.

The feelings of that moment will never be forgotten. As I write this book, I've taken well more than 100 deer, about half of them whitetails. None will ever compare with the first, which is as it should be.

The biggest buck taken from our large group of editors was killed by a lady editor who made a dandy shot. It was her first deer hunt!

MAY I HELP YOU GET
TO YOUR TREESTAND, SIR?

Every now and then I figure I'm owed an easy whitetail hunt to make up for all the frustrating and miserable hunts I've had in the past. One of those fine experiences occurred around 1980, when a new *OUTDOOR LIFE* editor decided to hold a strategy meeting at a lovely plantation retreat in South Carolina. The new editor was wanting to acquaint himself with all his writers, and wanted a casual meeting place. Besides the meetings, we'd be able to hunt whitetails on the property.

I had no idea what to expect, but when a bunch of us drove up to the plantation, we were instantly impressed. Huge live oak trees that no doubt had seen the Civil War, stood outside a beautiful building that oozed Deep South charm. I could almost smell the grits, collard greens, and blackeyed peas.

Our group was big, numbering about 23. It included not only the New York editors who worked in our Manhattan office, but also the field people like myself. At the time, I was editor-at-large, and lived in Utah. When we walked in the door, we were greeted by a negro gentleman wearing a spotless white jacket. He immediately offered a libation while another man showed us to our rooms. If the new editor had any intentions of pampering us, he was doing pretty good so far.

Once settled, we met for cocktails, an unbelievable dinner, and then lots of small talk and big talk around the spacious fireplace. Most of the talk was about whitetail hunting rather than running the magazine. The editorial conferences would begin in the morning, after we got back from deer hunting. I liked the way the whole trip was put together. Hunting was the priority, which, of course, was as it should be.

By 5 a.m., after a huge breakfast, we headed for the hunting areas. We crowded into pickup trucks and were driven by chauffeurs into the pitch black southern woods.

When it was my turn to get out, the black man who drove us led the way to my treestand with his flashlight. The stand was about 10 yards from the road, and a comfortable ladder led to the platform. My guide held my rifle while I climbed, then followed and made sure everything was comfy. He whispered final instructions before leaving, suggesting where the deer might come from.

This was standard operating procedure for southern hunting on large private land holdings. My treestand overlooked a lush grassy field cut out of a heavily timbered forest. Deer fed extensively in the green fields, and visited during the night, early in the morning, and late in the afternoon.

The hunting mode couldn't have been any simpler or easier. It wasn't really hunting per se, but a shoot. You waited for a deer to come to you, and made your move. No part of the grassy field was farther than 200 yards.

Of course, there was plenty of competition among us to get the biggest buck. It was a friendly rivalry, but it was serious as well. A lot of pride was resting on the biggest buck's antlers.

As I stood there in the dark, waiting for the birth of a new day, I thought about the unbelievably liberal hunting regulations in the south. In South Carolina, at least in the area we hunted, there was no limit on bucks! That's right, you read it correctly — you could shoot all the bucks you wanted. If you saw 10 a day, you could shoot all 10. They didn't have to be tagged; all you did was load them up in your truck and take them home. I believe that regulation applied for all of South Carolina, or most of it. The hunt I'm retelling here occurred about 10 years ago, but I'm told the regulations are still the same as I write this book in 1992.

The landowner of the property we hunted requested that we shoot one buck a day. Shucks — we were really being denied!

It was just getting light when two deer appeared in the gray morning mist. They had just walked out of the woods, and were about 60 yards away.

My binoculars identified one as a spike buck, and I waited until it was lighter before I lowered the boom. The little buck, and I mean little, hit the ground instantly.

I dragged the deer off the field, and dressed it at the edge of the woods. A couple hours later, the truck pulled up, and the black man looked at the tiny deer that I'd dragged to the road.

"Nice buck," he said, as he stooped over to lift it into the truck.

Nice buck? I thought he was kidding, and looked for a trace of a smile. There wasn't any.

Then the gentleman made a startling discovery. "Suh," he said, "you CLEANED this here buck. You ain't s'posed to do that, suh. We does it at the cleanin' shed."

I made some excuse for forgetting about the field dressing procedure, but I'm not used to letting a deer sit around with its innards intact. All my life I've gutted every animal immediately after the kill. If there was a delay, it was simply to take a few photos.

When we arrived at the cleaning shed, we learned that four other bucks had been taken. Three were spikes, the other a small three point. On the scales, my buck weighed 42 pounds. I was amazed; perhaps that's the reason you can shoot so many. You could polish off a deer at one big Sunday dinner.

After showers and lunch, we got down to business and had a meeting. Then the folks who hadn't gotten a deer went back out to make an evening hunt.

The next morning I was in another treestand, and the events of the day were a repeat of the first. Ten minutes after shooting light I put another spike buck down. Once again I field dressed it, and once again the guide fussed about me doing it.

When we pulled up to the cleaning shed, I saw a bunch of people staring at the ground, obviously looking at something interesting. As I approached, I saw a dandy 10-point buck lying there. It was a very good animal, far superior to the other bucks we'd taken.

"Who got it?" I asked immediately.

"Me", the lady said. "Would you believe it?"

What a surprise. Two of the six female editors in our group opted to hunt. Neither had hunted deer before, and in fact, neither had fired a high-powered rifle. The day we arrived, they practiced shooting with borrowed rifles.

The fact that the biggest buck of the hunt went to a first-time hunter, and a woman at that, was delightful.

As we walked back to the lodge, one of the hunters grumbled something to the effect that the lady would probably never kill a bigger buck the rest of her life. The buck had come too easy; now she was spoiled.

"You ever kill one that big, George?"

George, who indeed had hunted most of his life, grumbled some more. At that point, I think he was about to say to heck with deer hunting.

GET OFF YOUR HORSE BEFORE YOU SHOOT

I'd always wanted to be a hunting guide. To me, that's a crowning achievement, one that suggests that you're skilled enough to lead another hunter in his quest for game. My chance came in 1965, while I worked as a forester in Price, Utah, a coal mining town that is surrounded by sensational western mountains and scenery. As a district forester for the state, my region stretched from the Wyoming border in the north to the Arizona border in the south, encompassing one-third of the entire state. My job was to suppress forest fires and to advise ranchers on timber management programs, forest plantations, and other projects relating to timber and wildlife.

A rancher owned an absolutely beautiful chunk of real estate in the south Book Cliffs area, a high plateau covered with quaking aspen glades, douglas fir forests, dense oak stands, and sagebrush expanses. During deer season each year he ran a hunting outfit, and annually took on a couple dozen hunters, most of whom easily killed big bucks. Those that didn't either had a vision problem or were horrid shots.

I had helped the outfitter on some forestry programs, and when he asked if I'd like to guide for him during my vacation, I quickly agreed. I wouldn't be able to hunt the property until the last couple days, and that depended on all the clients filling their tags. My compensation would be $15 a day, plus whatever tip the client cared to offer. I was more interested in the experience than the money, though I'll admit that any cash would be welcome, given the fact that I was just out of college and struggling to pay bills. One of those bills was a $15 monthly payment I made on a Winchester shotgun that I'd purchased on a time payment plan. It took me a year to complete the payments. I also recall a time when my paycheck was late and all I had was a quarter. My coal supply ran out, and since it was dead winter and bitterly cold, I took my 25 cents to a coal yard and bought a sack of coal. That's being broke.

The hunting strategy on the ranch was fairly easy. I drove a jeep through the aspens, and when we spotted a good buck or two, I let the designated hunter out and continued driving down the road. If the plan worked, the deer watched us and not the hunter who was making the stalk. After a day or two, bucks wised up quickly and didn't hang around very long when a vehicle appeared. That's when we hiked through the draws and ridges, but the hunt wasn't very physical because most of the area was on a plateau except for some fairly deep canyons.

One of my fondest hunts was with G. Howard Gillelan, who was at the time bowhunting editor for OUTDOOR LIFE. I was thrilled to meet Howard, because a couple of my pieces had been published in OUTDOOR LIFE. I desperately wanted to be a full-time hunting writer, and I was anxious to meet a real live person who actually did it.

As it turned out, Howard was a gentleman, a fun companion, and an excellent hunter. Our hunt was during bow season in August, and bachelor groups of big bucks were everywhere. Howard constantly allowed other hunters in the party the opportunity to stalk a buck when it was his turn. Finally, after all the hunters scored, Howard started hunting seriously. Unfortunately, there were so many bucks around that it was almost impossible to get up on one. Howard wanted to arrow one fair and square by still hunting, and didn't care to use the vehicle. I was impressed with his ethics, and respected his attitude.

Finally, on the last day of the hunt, I pointed Howard toward a good spot while I went to check out a draw that had been lightly hunted. I located a giant buck feeding in an aspen patch, and slipped away unseen, making a bee-line for Howard.

When I found him, he was standing over a big doe that he'd shot squarely through the heart. He'd given up on bucks, and was looking for a good piece of venison. By the time I field dressed the doe, got her loaded in the rig, and hustled back over to the buck, the big deer was gone. At the time, bowhunters could take two deer of any sex, but Howard went home only with the doe.

Later he wrote a feature in OUTDOOR LIFE, called "Too Many Bucks." I was tickled to read it, because it was an excellent account of a great hunt.

When our clients were back in the lodge after hunting hours, the other guides and I worked on deer carcasses long into the night. Because August nights are warm, we skinned, boned, and cooled the deer on the evening of the day they were killed. Deer taken in August are superb eating, but the meat must be quickly chilled.

Another memorable hunt occurred while I guided for the outfitter, this time during rifle season. It seemed that a trio of hunters wanted to hunt in Desolation Canyon along the Green River. The outfitter told them that the area was essentially winter range, and there would be few bucks in the canyon during the rifle season in mid-October. The hunters were determined to hunt the area, and convinced the outfitter to set up a hunt.

Another guide and I took five saddle horses and five packhorses loaded with grub and gear from the lodge down to the canyon. To get there, we had to descend the cliffs along a treacherous trail that was several miles long. The hunters would fly in via a small airplane that would land in the canyon along the river.

The pilot of that plane was a local man whose skills as a pilot were legendary. It was said that he was the only man who would dare land a plane in Desolation Canyon. To make the landing, he had to enter the canyon, fly in it along all the nasty curves and bends, and finally put the plane down on a short sandy strip.

I was glad I was riding the horse, no matter how steep or dangerous the trail. No way would I ever get in that plane.

When the other guide and I got to the river, we repaired the corral and turned the horses in. Then we set up tents and prepared dinner. Another chore was to clear a strip for the plane to land. We dragged away driftwood, rocks, and other debris, and marked the strip with ribbons. Then we started a smoky fire so the pilot could check wind direction.

Dinner was about ready when I heard a drone from down the

canyon. Suddenly the plane appeared, standing on one wing as it rounded a terrible bend. Finally it leveled out and landed easily on the strip.

Two of the men inside were obviously amazed to be alive when they got out. They appeared to be badly shaken, and I recall one of them muttering something to the effect that it would be a cold day in hell before he'd fly in that thing again.

I took an instant dislike to the third man. He immediately complained about the cozy camp that I thought we'd set up, and was surly and obnoxious. He didn't appear to be unhappy with the plane ride, however. As it turned out, it was the only aspect of the hunt he was satisfied with.

I cooked thick steaks over a campfire that first night. He sarcastically instructed me to cook his steak EXACTLY seven minutes per side, and wanted the meat held 11 inches over the flame. I dearly wanted to tell him he reminded me of the south end of a northbound horse, but I kept my mouth shut. I liked my job and wanted to keep it until the deer season ran out.

He also complained about morning meals. I'm a pretty fair hand at cooking, but it was impossible to make his flapjacks the way he wanted them. They were either too doughy or too well-done. The other two hunters, on the other hand, were pleased with the food and were gentlemen all the way around.

The whiner immediately moaned and groaned over the poor hunting. We hunted hard, but saw only does, fawns, and a few small bucks. The hero said he'd seen one fair buck, but he couldn't get off the horse in time for a shot. Lucky for me, the other guide had the bad egg, and I had the two nice guys.

During one campfire conversation, the complainer asked if he could shoot off the horse if he saw another good buck. The other guide and I were aghast, and told the man that the only horses you could shoot off of lived in Hollywood. We were hunting in the wild west, not Universal Studios.

As the man continued to whine about the hunting, we reminded him that the outfitter told him that it was too early for the migration. There were a few good bucks in the canyon, but the majority were still up high.

One morning, when I woke up, I turned one of my boots upside down and shook it before putting it on. I don't know why I did it; something just told me to. A big juicy black widow spider popped out onto my sleeping bag, and I suddenly became an unhappy camper.

I was not in a great mood that day, what with the spider's presence and the complainer's terrible attitude. He'd put a damper on the rest of the party, and morale was lousy.

My spirits were lifted immediately, however, after hearing news of the day's hunt from the other guide when he and the bad guy returned to camp. It seemed that a nice buck showed up, and Mr. Wonderful took a shot from atop his horse. Predictably and happily, the horse reared up, and bucked off the hunter who landed squarely on his derriere. He wasn't hurt, but his pride was demolished. I laughed my fool head off in private after the guide recounted the incident.

Around the campfire that night, the whiner bitterly complained that he couldn't possibly go home without a deer. He said his wife would be furious at him for spending all that money and not getting anything to show for it. I secretly decided that he and his wife were probably made for each other. Sounded like a real unique couple.

I suggested we finish the hunt by riding back up onto the plateau where the big bucks lived. When we got to the lodge, we'd radio the pilot and tell him to cancel the return flight out of the canyon.

The complainer wouldn't have it, and told the four of us to go. He'd stay in the canyon by himself and fly out on the plane. We were so fed up with him that we agreed, even his companions. We broke camp, left him and his tent and some grub, and headed out for the top.

Several hours later, when we were just about to the rim, we spotted a pair of dandy bucks in the aspens. The two hunters pulled their rifles from the scabbards, drew beads, and put both bucks down. They were as delighted as the guide and I were, and we headed to the lodge with great stories to tell.

We learned later that the other hunter didn't get a deer, and I wished I could have seen his face when he learned that his pals had scored. I bet he said to heck with deer hunting in Desolation Canyon, and maybe he said to heck with deer hunting for good. One thing is for sure — he wouldn't be missed, at least not by the four of us who shared camp with him.

A pair of nice muley bucks.

A MELODY ON THE MOUNTAIN

The Wyoming mountain was a steep affair, rising high out of a sagebrush valley. It offered a respectable challenge to climb its slopes, but big muley bucks were reputed to live on it. Since I like hunting big muley bucks, I made the decision to climb it.

I left my pickup in the valley long before daybreak, and intended on hiking to the top, slowly working my way up in the brush and trees. I'd watch the several game trails that contoured around the mountain as I climbed.

I saw several deer as shooting light arrived, including a half-dozen bucks, but none wore antlers that had spreads much over 24 inches. I passed on all of them, hoping for one of the 30-inchers that lived in the area.

While slowly working up through the trees, I saw a buck staring at me through the foliage. I knew he was a mature animal, because I could see the fork of one antler. It appeared to be a hefty fork, but the rest of the rack was obscured by pinon branches.

The buck was rock-still. I believe he figured he was safe because he was hidden in the brush, but I knew he wouldn't hang around long. Sooner or later he'd take off.

I took a couple steps up the mountain, trying to position myself in a better vantage point. The buck decided to head out, and disappeared in the trees. At one point I caught a glimpse of his rack. It appeared to be rather wonderful, and well within the 30-inch category, but I had no clear shot at the animal.

Working my way across the precarious slope, I picked up the buck's track. When he rounded a bend, he'd gone straight up the mountain. I decided to follow.

I'd never been on the top of the mountain before, and I wasn't looking forward to the climb. I'd always wanted to climb it to see what was up there, and the buck gave me plenty of motivation to do so. I didn't have any hope of seeing him again, but you never know unless you try. It was possible he crossed the top and bedded down on the other side. I might very well get another look at him.

It was a miserable climb. I went straight up a clay slope, because it was the only one that offered a route. Most of the slopes were circled by a vertical eight-foot band of rock, requiring an extension ladder or rock-climbing gear to negotiate.

I'd climb up two steps and fall back one. In one place I made 10 feet, but slid back down 15 feet. For the most part, my cumulative progress was negative, but little by little I gained yardage.

As my elevation increased, so did my observation potential. It was still early enough for deer to be moving, and I saw several on the slopes across and below me, but they were does, fawns, and small bucks.

It took me a full two hours before I got close to the top. I'd given up on following the buck's specific trail, because he went up places that gave me the shudders. I could, however, see his general trail where his hooves left fresh marks in the mountainside. When I topped out, I'd find his tracks again and follow.

I was drenched with sweat, and aching from head to toe when the top was a few yards away. I was so hot, in fact, that I heard music softly playing. The sun had really gotten to me, I supposed, and I sat down to take a break. My brain must really have been fried. Music? Up here on top of the world?

Presently I got up to hike the rest of the short distance, and I heard the music again. It seemed to be coming from the very top of the mountain, just out of sight.

By now I was mystified. Had I fallen and broken my neck and passed on to the Great Hunting Spot In The Sky? Was I heading for St. Peter?

As I stumbled up to the top, the music grew louder. It was strange music to be coming from the Great Gate. Instead of something that you'd expect, like a nice hymn being sung by the Mormon Tabernacle Choir, it was a song being sung by the Beach Boys.

Imagine my surprise when I looked over the top and saw a new Chevy pickup parked on the rim. A guy and gal were sitting in the truck; he was peering through a spotting scope, she was looking bored. I was looking mad.

The man saw me, and was astounded at my presence.

"Where'd you come from?" he asked.

"Down there," I answered, gesturing over the rim.

"You CLIMBED that side?" he asked with a great deal of disbelief in his voice.

"Yeah," I answered simply.

"You're kidding," the music man said.

"See that blue dot down there?" I stated. "That's my pickup truck."

"Man, you Utah guys are crazy, but why didn't you drive up here like I did?" he suggested.

"Didn't know the road was there," I answered.

When I wiped the sweat from my brow, the man offered me an ice-cold Pepsi. I accepted, and the offering swept away the nasty feelings I had toward him at the moment.

"Did you see the big buck that headed up here?" I asked.

"No," he answered, "must not have been watching in the right direction."

By the look he shot his lady friend, I had an idea that they weren't looking at much of anything before I'd arrived. I guessed they might have been occupied, engaged in other matters.

After cooling off, I headed back down the mountain, sliding much of the way down. I made a decision right then to never again climb a stupid mountain until I checked to see if there was a road on the rim.

I wasn't mad at the Wyoming guy, though. The Pepsi hit the spot, and besides, I like the Beach Boys.

WHEN THE TEXAS GOATS CAME TO DINNER

Murry Burnham is the kind of guy you can't help liking — a lot. He's a shy, quiet man, who never has a bad word for anyone. If you've been an avid hunter over the years, you've no doubt heard of Burnham Brothers calls. They include predator, waterfowl, turkey, deer, elk calls, and lots of others, but the predator calls are best known.

In fact, several decades ago, Murry's Dad invented the first predator call. It imitated a rabbit in distress, and when news of the call got out, it was met with plenty of skepticism. I was one of the early disbelievers, until I called coyotes on my very first try. That was back in 1961, when I was a forestry student at Utah State University.

Murry's father picked up the rabbit distress concept when he heard a jackrabbit squealing loudly. Upon investigating, he discovered the animal caught in a fence, and moments later two foxes dashed in to see what the commotion was all about. Mr. Burnham correctly deduced that the foxes were attracted to the squalling rabbit, and when he imitated the sound, he was startled at the reaction from all sorts of predators — coyotes, bobcats, foxes, even mountain lions.

A small shop at his home was soon turned into a predator call factory. The first models were roughly made, but they were slowly redesigned. Soon the hunting community around the nation was on to predator calls, and a new industry began to thrive and grow.

Murry and his brother took over the business from their Dad afterward and turned it into a successful enterprise. Everyone acquainted with Murry knows that he hates the business end of the company, and would much rather be in the woods.

I've been around lots of hunters. In my job as a hunting writer, I've been fortunate to have met many of the best woodsmen in the country. I'm serious when I say this — Murry is at the top of the list. He has the ability to think like the quarry he pursues. More often than not, he returns to camp with game rather than tales and excuses. Murry is the kind of hunter who leaves camp several hours before daybreak with a couple apples in his jacket pocket. He returns to camp long after dark when dinner is cold and everyone else is ready for bed.

Murry introduced me to my first Texas hunt many years ago. It was a turkey hunt, which ended up successful, thanks to Murry's expert calling. A couple years later, I returned to Texas to hunt deer. Among Murry's skills, he was considered to be one of the top deer rattlers in the country, and was one of the first to try it.

I'd heard about rattling long ago. In fact, anyone who hunts whitetails and reads about them has GOT to know about rattling. Hundreds of articles have been written about the method over the years; rattling is a household word among whitetail hunters, especially in the south, and especially in Texas where it seems to work best.

My first Texas deer hunt with Murry was an eye opener, demonstrating once again that until you see something with your very own eyes, you have a hard time believing it. I knew rattling worked. Too many people I respected told me it did. But until that hunt, I'd never seen it done.

Murry and I hunted out of his ranch, and before sunrise the first day we were walking toward a brushy basin. The sun was just making an appearance when Murry began rattling. With an antler in each hand, he whacked them together, and then kept rubbing them so they twisted and ground, simulating two bucks fighting.

The first buck came so fast I couldn't believe it. I spotted him approaching 200 yards away, and he was on a dead run, making a beeline for Murry. I was so entranced with the scenario that I didn't raise my rifle. The buck kept coming, but quit about 75 yards out. Then

Murry with one of many big whitetails he's rattled up. In my opinion, he's the best in the business.

Murry did something unbelievable. He held the two antlers high over his head and clacked them together in full view of the buck. Then he kicked a big rock loose near his foot. It went rolling down the slope, and the buck darted in even closer.

The deer was a modest 8-pointer, and I let him go. This rattling business was too much fun. I wanted to watch as many deer react as possible, and would shoot only if a brute of a buck came in. None did, but plenty of other bucks did. I went home without venison, but with plenty of vivid memories, and a whole lot of new admiration for Murry.

My next Texas hunt with Murry was one of the most hilarious hunts I'd ever been on. A member of our hunting party was born and raised in the Louisiana bayous, and he had all the qualities of a full-blown cajun. His dialect was about as severe as could be (which pleased me immensely, because I think Louisiana, its traditions, inhabitants, and customs are fascinating), and he was a funny man with lots of jokes and witty remarks.

It seemed that our cajun campmate had become involved in our hunt after a telephone conversation with Murry several weeks prior to the hunt. The cajun claimed he had a trap that would catch catfish by the buckets, and wanted Murry to include the trap in his Burnham Brothers hunting catalog. In his casual, friendly way, Murry invited the cajun to bring his traps and hunt deer at the same time. It seemed there were a couple tanks on Murry's ranch that held catfish. (In Texas, a "tank" is a small reservoir or pond).

The cajun lived in the bayou country and caught catfish for a living. He was also an expert cook, and I didn't get very far from him in the kitchen, because I love to cook and am always willing to learn something new.

The catfish traps worked. The cajun baited them with rotten, awful smelling cheese. Though the catfish were quite small, running eight to nine inches, the cajun skinned them so fast I was amazed. He claimed he'd won some catfish skinning contests; I didn't doubt it.

He made a delicious dish called catfish couvignon. I got the recipe, and one of my greatest regrets in this life is that I lost it, and have never been able to duplicate the recipe since, though I've tried others.

The first morning of the hunt was quite an experience. I thought I'd seen a lot in deer woods around the country — this incident was most interesting.

Before leaving camp, Murry told me where my stand was. I was to head down the fence a half mile, turn left at the intersection of the first fence, and walk to the fifth post, which was under my stand. Of course, all this travel was in the black of night, so I made my way with a small flashlight. I had arrived in camp the evening before, and wasn't able to orient myself with the area.

I climbed up into the stand, which was fairly typical for Texas. It was a metal tower, with a totally enclosed five foot square platform, complete with a comfortable seat. Small openings allow you to poke your rifle barrel out, and there was no problem with a rest — you simply used the window sill.

Towers like these are standard in Texas deer country. They're usually located along a fence line where you have visibility, or at the edge of an opening or sendero. A sendero is a path bulldozed through the brush, which is made expressly for the purpose of improving visibility.

Because of the brush, towers are used to elevate the hunter to where the quarry could be seen. Lately, Texas hunters have been taking a whopping number of 400,000 whitetails annually. I'd wager that 75 percent of those deer are shot from towers.

As daybreak arrived, I saw all sorts of critters moving about, but no bucks. A few does and fawns slipped through the brush, and there were plenty of doves and quail around.

I was totally immersed in the splendor of that lovely awakening Texas morning when a sudden loud metallic noise erupted from close by and scared me out of my wits. I looked out the back of my tower, and saw a contraption on a tripod partially screened by brush. It appeared to be some sort of device that was spewing something on the ground.

Moments later, doves, quail, songbirds, turkeys, and deer rushed to the spot. It didn't take a rocket scientist to figure out what was going on. The contraption was a feeder, set up to attract deer to my stand.

I didn't know whether to be mad or amused; finally I chose the latter. Baiting deer is a big (and legal) practice in Texas. (When I talked to the chief biologist with the Texas Game Department, he told me that baiting was necessary to get the required harvest. There are so many deer in Texas that huge numbers need to be thinned each year. Baiting is an important means of obtaining that harvest.) If you drive about in Texas deer country during deer season, you'll see dozens of roadside signs advertising corn for bait. It's big business, and no doubt adds a boost to the local economy each year.

No legal bucks showed up at the feeder, just a spike and a bunch of does and fawns. That particular area required bucks to be forked-horn or better, but I wasn't about to lower the boom on anything but a decent buck. The spike continued to eat up the grain.

Big bucks seemed to be elusive the next couple days. No one in the party saw any. In the meantime, we continued to eat catfish and had plenty of laughs listening to our cajun friend.

On the third morning, Murry put me and the cajun in towers that were about 600 yards apart. Each tower overlooked a big opening, and Murry applied a generous contribution of corn in the openings. The idea, of course, was for the corn to draw in a buck.

I sat in my tower, waiting for something to happen, when I saw movement in the cajun's opening. With my binoculars I saw five billy goats gobbling up the corn. Suddenly the cajun appeared from the tower, and ran toward the goats, screaming, waving his hat, and jumping up

Murry with a fine Colorado muley. He's just as skilled at hunting muleys as he is whitetails.

and down. Though I was 600 yards away, I could clearly hear the invectives turning the air blue. I couldn't help but to laugh, and I laughed so hard I was afraid the cajun would hear me.

Finally, with the goats run off, the cajun returned to his tower. Fifteen minutes later, the goats came back, and once again the cajun was out of his tower and running after the goats. This time he was more animated in his actions, and his cussing was louder. The cajun was a very short man, and I was thoroughly amused at the scenario, laughing harder than ever.

The goats were a tenacious lot, and returned a third time. The cajun had had it, and stomped away toward the road, but not before chasing the goats a final time and throwing his hat at them.

The scene generated the heartiest laugh I had that year. I remarked something about the goats at the dinner table that night, and the cajun took it in good spirits. He said to heck with deer hunting, at least at Murry's ranch, and I'm not sure if he ever returned for a bout with Texas's deer.

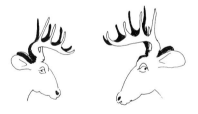

Janette with her first buck. I wrote a story about it with ease, because it came straight from the heart.

A BUCK FOR JANETTE

NOTE — This chapter was printed as a feature article in OUTDOOR LIFE. Unbeknown to author Jim Zumbo, the OUTDOOR LIFE editors submitted the article in six national writing contests sponsored by the Outdoor Writer's Association of America. You can imagine Zumbo's surprise when the article took 5 first place awards and one second place.

My two daughters and I stood on the ridge and looked down into the juniper forest across the canyon. My binoculars helped me spot a doe and two fawns lying under a tree, and I glassed intently for a buck that might be hidden nearby. After 10 minutes, I gave up and sat down on a ledge, and instructed Judi and Janette to do likewise. Perhaps a buck would become restless and move around.

"Can I use your binoculars, Dad?" 14-year-old Judi asked in a whisper.

I passed them to her and relaxed as she scanned the canyon below us. It was 10 a.m. and the weather was superb — too good for hunting. The temperature was about 60 degrees, and there wasn't a cloud in the brilliant blue Utah sky.

"I see a deer, Dad." Judi suddenly announced, "and it's a buck!"

I looked down to where the binoculars were aimed and saw two deer — a forkhorn and a doe.

"Don't move," I instructed. "They don't see us and I want Janette to find a good rest."

I eased over to a nearby cornice and wadded my jacket into a ball, watching the deer as I moved. I motioned to Janette to slip over to the jacket and use it for a rifle rest, but the deer quickly disappeared in the high sagebrush. Assuming they bedded down, we stood motionless and waited.

I was nervous and excited, because I badly wanted Janette to kill a buck. It would be the first for my 20-year-old daughter, and I had been feeling like a failure as a father. A few weeks before hunting season, Janette told me she wanted to hunt deer. I was mildly surprised, because, in the past she was content to just go along on the hunt and hike around, or read in camp. She and her brother, Dan, had accompanied me on deer and elk hunts since they were 10 years old. Many times they followed dutifully behind me as I slipped along a deer trail, and every now and then I had to turn and bawl them out for making too much noise, or fighting to see who walked directly behind me.

Janette never winced or showed displeasure as I field dressed game, and always seemed interested in the process. More than once I identified each vital organ to the children as I cleaned birds, rabbits, deer, and elk.

Although Janette passed her hunter safety test when she was 14 , she had never hunted, and never expressed an interest in doing so. That's why I was surprised when she announced she wanted to kill a deer.

As we sat there on the ridgetop, waiting for the buck to appear, I recalled the conversation I'd had with Janette a month ago.

"You really want to hunt deer?" I said to her when she asked about going on a hunt.

"Yes," she answered. " I always wanted to hunt."

"You have?" I responded incredulously. "For how long?"

"Ever since I was old enough," she replied quietly. "But you always took Dan."

"Why didn't you tell me," I said.

"Oh, I don't know," she answered. "I guess I thought I'd always be too much of a bother."

Janette must have sensed my feelings. I was upset with myself, frustrated because I never knew my daughter's desire to hunt.

"Don't feel bad, Dad," she smiled. "It's no big deal."

It WAS a big deal, though. I'd failed her, and it took far too long to find out. My daughter was a lovely woman now, talented, intelligent, and mature. For too many years I'd neglected her, always assuming she wasn't interested in actively participating in our hunts.

Although I don't consider myself a male chauvinist, I was painfully guilty of ignoring Janette in favor of Dan. As I perceived it, hunting was a man's sport, and, in my mind, it was natural for me to expend all my time and effort on my son.

After Janette and I had that talk, I recalled several outings we'd had. When she was 14, I took her along on a Wyoming mule deer hunt. The two of us walked a dozen miles that day, but she never complained.

Another time, she and I stalked a buck deer in a Utah forest, crawling 100 yards on our bellies to do so. When I killed the buck she was as excited as I was.

It was Dan, however, who received all my attention. When he was 3, I carried him on my shoulders when I trained my German Shorthair over live pheasants. I gave him an air rifle when he was 10, a .22 at 12, a shotgun at 14, and a rifle at 16. When he turned 14, I took him deer hunting in neighboring Colorado because the Utah minimum age is 16. And so it went.

Now it was time to undo all those wrongs. I prayed for the buck to appear, and I fervently hoped Janette wouldn't miss if she got a shot. A miss might turn her off for good.

As I glassed the sagebrush-choked canyon bottom, I heard rocks falling from the steep slope just below us. We all heard the noise at the same time, and I turned to see the buck and doe slowly walking up the mountain toward us. The deer hadn't spotted us, but it would only be a matter of time. We were in a clump of sparse brush and weren't concealed very well.

Janette eased the rifle to her shoulder and looked at me quizzically. I knew what was on her mind. She'd accompanied me on too many hunts.

"No time to find a rifle rest," I whispered, "and we don't dare move. You'll have to shoot him offhand. Let him get as close as possible."

The deer were only 75 yards away when an errant breeze apparently alerted them. The doe tossed her head up and looked directly at us. The buck stopped instantly and also spotted us.

Time seemed to stand still as Janette drew a bead through the scope. Several thoughts raced through my mind. She was using my .30/06 and I feared she would flinch as she squeezed the trigger. Or perhaps she'd suffer a case of buck fever and blow the shot. Or worse yet, she might wound the buck, requiring a careful pursuit in the steep, dangerous canyons.

Several seconds passed, but Janette didn't fire. I was beside myself with anxiety, but I didn't say a word. Suddenly the doe snorted and made a quick bound up the slope. The buck took a short, nervous step, and it was his final act.

The rifle cracked and the deer fell to the ground. He lay still, and I knew he belonged to my daughter.

Normally I don't show much outward emotion when an animal is claimed, but I couldn't help myself this time. I jumped around like a fool and hugged Janette as we hurried over to the fallen buck. Both girls were wide-eyed and excited as we approached the deer, and I fumbled with my camera, unable to compose myself for the ensuing photo session.

After instructing Janette to pose with the buck, I observed her carefully for some show of feelings. She was trembling and her eyes were a bit teary, but I detected no misgivings in her attitude.

"Do you feel badly about killing the deer?" I asked.

"No, Dad," she answered. "It's young and fat, and will be good eating. Besides, there's no easy way for a deer to die. It could starve, get hit by a car, die from a horrible disease, or be killed by a cougar or coyotes."

I was relieved that my daughter had no regrets. Her philosophy about taking an animal's life was an intelligent one, but it wasn't an attitude she'd come up with herself. I taught the children about the natural world — the real natural world; not the one portrayed in absurd movies and T.V. shows.

Our family lived in New York state for a period of time while the children were growing up. Each year I managed to hang a whitetail buck from the maple tree alongside our house, and occasionally some

Judi and I pose with Janette. I didn't make the same mistake with Judi. She began hunting deer as soon as she was old enough.

neighborhood children made comments to my youngsters about me killing deer. I explained hunting to Dan and Janette, and they were satisfied with my viewpoint. Because they accompanied me on hunts when they were young, they had a first-hand look at the sport.

Unfortunately, most kids these days have no opportunity to go hunting. Worse, boys are almost exclusively initiated into the hunting fraternity.

When girls do hunt with their fathers, it's usually because that particular family has no sons. Plenty of men have told me, "I don't have any boys, so my daughter is my hunting buddy."

That's too bad, but I understand the attitude. I was guilty of it myself until Janette finally told me she wanted to hunt.

I won't make the same mistake with Judi. She passed her hunter safety test and hunted cottontails with me last year.

Like Janette, Judi expressed no remorse when she killed her first animal. She ran over to the fatally hit but still-kicking rabbit, plucked it out of the snow, and proudly hoisted it up for me to see. She killed two more that day, and she helped me skin and dress them when the hunt was over.

To be sure, daughters require more understanding and patience than sons, when it comes to hunting. Girls are expected to play with dolls, boys play with soldiers and toy guns.

They're programmed that way from an early age. It's easy and natural for a boy to make the transition from toy guns to real guns, but it's more of an effort to introduce girls to firearms if they haven't been exposed to them during pre-adolescence.

It's wrong to think that girls and women are automatically turned off by hunting. A good pal of mine recently took his wife on a Wyoming antelope hunt. He was apprehensive, because this was her first hunt. She had never fired a gun in her life until he prepared for the trip. Born in Philadelphia, she was raised a city girl and had no outdoor experience. My pal's worries were in vain. His wife not only killed a buck antelope with a well placed shot, but she bemoaned the fact that she didn't have a deer tag as well.

Another friend moved West a few years ago, and took his Connecticut-reared wife along on an antelope hunt. She was impressed, and quickly learned how to shoot. Now she's his constant hunting companion.

Hunting has long been thought to be solely a man's sport. It isn't. It's important to recognize that women, no matter what age, have many of the same outdoor interests as men. You might have to nudge your daughter, wife, or girlfriend to develop a latent urge that would never surface without your encouragement, but it's worth it.

My daughters will always be my hunting pals. As I write this, my youngest daughter, Angie, who is 12, wants to shoot her first rabbit this winter.

I can't wait to take her.

THE DUMBEST HIGHWAY OF ALL

When I lived in Vernal, Utah, for about a dozen years, I commonly bought a nonresident Colorado license and hunted both states, since Vernal is only about 25 miles from the Colorado border. There wasn't any great advantage in hunting either state for deer. Both gave up some good bucks, but both were crowded with hunters, particularly on public land. I mean REALLY crowded, the kind of mob scene you'd expect in New York or California.

My first buck ever, which I discuss elsewhere in this book, was killed in Utah just a half mile from the Colorado border. The area, called Blue Mountain, was a frustrating place to hunt because Dinosaur National Monument occupies a good share of the real estate on Blue Mountain. The Monument, established many years ago to protect a concentrated deposit of dinosaur bones in Utah, had been enlarged when the government decided to add much of the Green and Yampa river corridors, as well as a lovely chunk of the top of Blue Mountain that offered a spectacular view of the rivers below.

I had no problem with enlargement of the monument, even though its lands are strictly closed to hunting, thanks to the policies of the National Park Service that manages our monuments. My problem was the road that led from the park headquarters at the bottom of Blue Mountain up to the scenic spot on top, a distance of some 20 to 25 miles. The Park Service built the road through BLM and private land, and prohibited hunters from parking along it to gain access to public hunting lands immediately adjacent to it.

In other words, if you wanted access to that side of Blue Mountain, you had to travel the park highway, and you could leave it only at infrequent gates. If you saw a big buck on BLM land next to the highway, you could not pull over, park your vehicle, and make a stalk on the buck. You couldn't hunt the area at all, because there was no access.

In some places, with good maps, you could exit the highway at one of the few gates that access public land, avoid private acreage and legally hunt on the public BLM lands, but those areas were few and far between. The highway confined you to a corridor you could not have access from, even though the highway crossed BLM land. What made me additionally unhappy was the fact that the old road, before the highway, provided perfectly fine access. You could hunt from it to your heart's content. It was a dirt road, and I vaguely remember driving on it when I killed my first buck on Blue Mountain in the early 1960's.

When I lived in Vernal, I made it a personal commitment to outwit the park rangers that ran up and down the highway with their green vehicles and red lights, harassing hunters and enforcing the stupid law that denied access from the highway. With the best maps I could find, and by using colored pencils, I identified all the BLM public land, private land, and access points. I guess you might say I defied any park ranger to confront me, because I had been legally hunting on BLM land every step of the way, and my vehicle was legally parked off the highway.

I killed some fine muleys by using those maps, and I never had a confrontation with a Park Ranger, either. Actually, I don't have a general dislike for Park Service personnel. Most of them are pretty fine folks. In fact, as I write this I'm sitting in my Wyoming home two dozen miles from Yellowstone Park. I know some right friendly personnel in Yellowstone, and I suppose the people who run Dinosaur National

Monument are pretty nice, too. It's the damnable road that gets to me. It'll always be a pet peeve.

Another access problem is caused by private lands that block BLM government acreage. In many cases, you can resolve the dilemma by using a good map and walking only on public land. There's a particular chunk of land on Blue Mountain that a bunch of guys bought and immediately posted. The former landowner allowed hunting if you asked permission, but these new guys locked it up entirely. What they hadn't counted on was enterprising hunters gaining access to parcels of public land adjacent to their property by simply skirting their borders. I did it a number of times, and I ran into the landowners on several occasions. They were unhappy with my presence, but they couldn't do a thing about it. Their rights applied only to their property, not to the public BLM land that offered free hunting.

One of the biggest muley bucks I ever saw in my life was on Blue Mountain as I was hunting around the perimeter of the private land. I flushed him out of a pocket of junipers about 80 yards away, and he bounded through the sage, his huge rack of antlers swaying back and forth as he moved. Suddenly he stopped about 125 yards out and looked at me, remaining there for about 10 seconds. I was bowhunting at the time; all I could do was look and drool. He was an incredible animal, with a rack that easily spanned 35 inches in width. His tines were thick and deeply forked, and I was certain he'd rank high in the record book.

I hunted that buck the rest of bow season, and during rifle season the next several years. I never saw him again, but that's why he was so huge. He was without question an old buck, and had learned how to be a survivor.

Because the Colorado-Utah border divides Blue Mountain, there are lots of shenanigans among hunters. The Colorado season usually opens earlier than Utah's, so the Colorado hunters somehow miss seeing all those signs that indicate the state borders. Some hunters miss those signs so badly that they encroach a mile or two inside the wrong state. Shucks, many of those boys ought to pay more attention, but the fact of the matter is that they generally know precisely where they are. To them, it's a great bonus to hunt land that isn't quite open to hunting yet. Of course, Utah hunters have the same trouble seeing the Colorado signs, and they likewise manage to add a few hundred acres to their hunting area.

As you can imagine, game wardens have fits when this is going on. Now and then the wardens catch a few trespassers, but not very many. Actually, some of the hunters genuinely are unaware that they've crossed the line. There is no fence that indicates the borders on much of the mountain, and the signs aren't placed very close together. It's entirely possible to hunt and walk into a bordering state without knowing it.

One of my fondest hunts ever on Blue Mountain occurred when my son, Danny, killed his first buck on it after he reached legal hunting age. Danny killed the buck about two miles from where I got my first buck, but that's another story recounted elsewhere in this book.

A few years after Danny got that buck, we went back to the very spot where I got my first muley in 1962. I'd never been back to that canyon in 20 years, and wanted to have another look. To reach it, we had to park our pickup and hike through the sage a considerable distance.

When we got there, we split up, and soon afterward I heard a single shot from down in the canyon. I just knew that Danny had scored on a buck bigger than mine, and I'd be in for some teasing. That wasn't the case, however. Dan had taken a small buck, but he was quite content. He had a big grin when I walked up to him, and I couldn't help wondering if the little buck had some of the genes of the old mossyhorn I'd killed 20 years before. That was a nice thought.

A year later, Dan got another small buck on Blue Mountain, this time near the stupid park highway that I dislike so much. We did it legally, of course, and I was absolutely delighted when he got the buck. That highway, as you can probably tell, irritates me no end. It is unfair, and I'll no doubt go back to Blue Mountain one of these days just to once again foil the boys who patrol the road. As usual, I'll do it legally, just to satisfy myself another time.

I don't always get mad, sometimes I get even, and I'll always say to heck with that dumb highway.

SASKATCHEWAN'S GIANT BUCKS

Saskatchewan. The name rolls off the tongue with a touch of difficulty, but once said, it suggests some common perceptions.

Canada. Cold country. Royal Canadian Mounted Police. And, to astute hunters, monster whitetails.

It was the latter term that occupied my mind most of the way from my home in Wyoming to a place in that western Canadian province, a place reputed to be inhabited by some of the biggest whitetails in the world. For years I'd dreamed of hunting Saskatchewan, ever since I first learned through the Boone and Crockett book that the province produced more trophy whitetails than any other province or U.S. state. The latest record book shows that Minnesota has taken the lead in trophy whitetails, followed by Wisconsin, but Saskatchewan holds a strong third place.

As my pickup rolled north, I watched the landscape change from enormous rolling prairies and farms that stretched across the horizon, to stands of poplar, firs, spruces, and jackpines.

To us in the lower 48, that vegetation is called forests. To a Canadian, it's known as the bush.

The bush. A simple word, but one that implies unexplored frontiers, backwoods wildernesses where fur trappers and the hardiest hunters roam. The bush would be my hunting ground for a week, the spot where I hoped to see the biggest whitetail of my life.

A meat pole carries a nice bunch of Saskatchewan whitetails.

Weldon Parsons is the kind of man you'd be comfortable hunting the bush with. A native of British Columbia, he's lived in some of western Canada's most remote regions, including the Yukon. Parsons teaches wilderness survival in Saskatchewan, runs a trapline, and has just begun guiding hunters for whitetails. I was one of his first deer hunters, and I was ready for what the bush had to offer.

Accommodations were simple and comfortable. Hunters slept in a cabin next to Weldon's home, and were treated to superb meals cooked by Weldon's wife. There was no water or electricity, the water being pumped from a well, and light supplied by oil lamps and lanterns. Heat was produced by a woodstove, and meals were cooked on a stove fired by wood and coal. A Chippewa boy and a Cree girl, 9 and 12 years old respectively, were being raised within the family, and two sons who worked as hunting guides lived there as well.

I marveled at the closeness of the family unit, and the way they dealt with some of the material things that most of us take for granted. The Indian children, for example, were allowed to watch an occasional TV show when their homework was completed. A tiny TV that picked up only a couple of channels was hooked up to a six-volt battery. I wondered how many modern kids could cope with that arrangement for just a day, let alone year-round.

My hunt would run into the first week of December, which translates to cold. Real cold. I was prepared for it, and, as it turned out, the bitterly cold temperatures were a major problem.

I'm always amazed when some writers claim that snow offers quiet walking. Maybe I hunt on different kinds of snow than those folks. When snow lays on the ground overnight and sets up, it becomes a confounding nuisance, squeaking loudly as you walk. The colder the temperature, the louder it squeaks. To make matters worse, there's no solution, other than not to walk at all.

That was the case when Weldon and I entered the bush. Temperatures around O degrees Fahrenheit and colder made the snow an abomination. Deer heard us coming for a quarter mile away or more, quickly flushing unseen.

Saskatchewan laws restrict non-Canadian hunters to the northern part of the province. The southern off-limits region includes farmlands with adjacent brushy draws and wooded patches. Those spots hold enormous bucks, and most are taken early in the morning or late in the afternoon when the animals feed in fields.

With some exceptions, the northern region available to non-Canadians offered no such opportunity, though giant bucks are regularly taken from the forest. In the bush, whitetails had to be hunted on their terms, in woodlands that reminded me of Maine and northern New York.

Weldon and I wasted no time attacking the timber. Dressed in white clothing from neck to ankles (required by Saskatchewan law) we forged into the trees before opening light of the first day.

Our initial strategy was to check scrapes and tracks. Because it was early December, Weldon figured that much of the rut was over. In

The boys are having a little fun, but notice the body size of the bucks. Canadian whitetails are huge.

northern latitudes, breeding season starts and finishes much earlier than in the south.

Our first day afield seemed to reinforce Weldon's concerns. We found a few fairly active scrapes here and there, but the primary scrapes Weldon had watched all season showed no action.

Still hunting was our strategy most of the day, but the noisy snow was our undoing. We saw a few deer as they scooted away, but none of them wore antlers. Fresh tracks in the snow betrayed the presence of plenty of deer that flushed long before we could see or hear them. Now and then Weldon tried rattling, but nothing showed. His rattling efforts paid off consistently a couple weeks prior to my hunt, but that was two weeks ago.

The next day was more of the same. We checked scrapes, hoping to find active diggings that I could watch from a ground blind, but nothing looked very promising. I saw some huge scrapes that had been made a week or two before, but they were too old. Watching them would have been a shot in the dark. Again we tried rattling, but the strategy was uneventful.

We teamed up with another guide and his hunter the following day. Weldon and the other outfitter made a drive through a dense willow bottom while the hunter and I slowly walked each side of the bottom, staying just ahead of the drivers on ridgetops that bordered the valley. The drivers whacked trees with branches so we could keep ourselves properly positioned.

The moving drive produced several deer, including a good buck, but I didn't have a good enough look at him to make an evaluation. This wasn't the place to shoot a routine buck. By the size of some of the tracks I'd seen, I knew there were some truly giant whitetails in the vicinity. Several times I saw tracks almost the size of a spike bull elk's, but I never saw the bucks that made those prints.

The rest of the hunt was uneventful, though I'd seen a number of fine bucks. I'd have taken any of them on other hunts, but they weren't up to Saskatchewan's trophy buck standards.

One buck was bedded in deep powdery snow. He flushed in heavy timber, and stopped about 40 yards away. When he flushed I saw gleaming, heavy antlers through the brush, but neither Weldon nor I saw his rack well enough to make a determination. I saw the deer's four legs as he stood in the underbrush, but his rack was hidden. The buck finally

Weldon displays some very big shed antlers. Lots of large antlers are found each year.

bounded into the trees, offering no look at his antlers.

We saw several other bucks in the bush and in fields where they fed throughout the night. In some areas, farmlands are accessible to non-Canadian hunters, especially in places where the fields border the forest.

While I hunted with Weldon, several Canadians from British Columbia were included in our party. They scored 100 percent on very nice bucks, all of them taken from agricultural regions off-limits to non-Canadians.

It would be easy to imply that American hunters are discriminated against, being required to hunt the northern forest areas which offer tougher hunting. I saw enough, however, to know that the northern regions produce giant bucks, and I wasn't feeling sorry for myself.

According to Dave Brewster, Saskatchewan's Provincial Whitetail Biologist for the Wildlife Branch, trophy bucks come from every part of the province's whitetail habitat. Brewster believes that soil is an important factor in growing big deer, since soil translates to better feed. In that regard, many big bucks come from the farming areas, but feed isn't the only ingredient. In order to grow huge racks, deer must be several years old, and that's where the bush has an important edge. Because of the very limited hunter pressure and the forest cover, bucks are apt to live longer. On the negative side, winters are more severe in the bush country, sometimes causing extensive mortality.

During the six days I hunted the forest with Weldon, I never saw another hunter, and only an occasional man track. It was evident that few people entered the bush, and it was easy to understand why. Farm country is much easier to hunt, and deer are much more visible. There isn't any need for residents to hunt the bush when they can collect their deer in the open agricultural environment.

I'm convinced that Saskatchewan will continue to be a top producer of huge whitetails, and I'm not so sure the province shouldn't be ranked at the top of the record book, instead of third place.

Here's why. Many Canadians are not the least interested in scoring systems, and don't care to have antlers measured. I saw at least two Boone and Crockett-quality racks in restaurants, none of which were officially scored. Weldon introduced me to several farmers who had enormous antlers nailed to barn walls or in a garage or basement. I suspect that if all those ignored heads around the province were measured, Saskatchewan would have so many heads in the record book that every whitetail hunter in North America who cares about trophy bucks would be utterly amazed.

Saskatchewan is one place where you don't easily say to heck with deer hunting. The potential is too great for a giant buck. You never know when the buck of your dreams will show up.

Note — Weldon Parsons was involved in a terrible automobile accident the year after I hunted with him. In fact, he had some whitetail hunters in his vehicle when the accident occurred. At first, prospects for Weldon's full recovery were poor. Doctors said he'd be a quadriplegic. Miraculously, Weldon began making improvements that stymied doctors. He can now use a walker, and continues to improve.

Weldon rattles amidst the splendor of the Canadian bush country, a top spot for big whitetails.

I COULDN'T HAVE MISSED THAT BLACKTAIL

The hunt was hardly what I'd expected. Instead of dreary rain and soggy woods, the sun shone brightly on the tinder-dry forest. The fall climate in western Washington was definitely not living up to its usual pattern.

It was my first blacktail deer hunt, one that I'd anticipated for years. My pal Dan Boes, who runs a dental lab in Chehalis, Washington, agreed to line up a hunt with his friend Mark Wilson, a logger who loves to hunt big game, especially blacktails.

I told Dan at the outset that I had been looking for a place to hunt with the locals — no exclusive private lands or special favors. I'd passed up invitations to hunt blacktails on ranches with high success rates for big bucks; this hunt would be with the crowds.

Mark met me at a cafe early opening morning, and we headed for a forest owned by a large timber company. Though it was private land, the company allowed anyone to hunt, essentially offering public access. Because of the high fire danger, many woodlands were closed, forcing hunters onto the few areas that were left open. As I soon learned, my desire to hunt with crowds was about to materialize.

Opening morning strategy was routine. Mark drove to a landing where we had a good view of a clearcut. We parked the vehicle and found good vantage points.

When shooting light arrived, I glassed the thick vegetation with binoculars. After several minutes of searching, I saw four deer moving slowly in the brush, but none wore antlers.

A shot close by brought me to attention. Someone on the other side of the clearcut had fired, and I was pleased to learn later that a young boy had taken his first buck, a small spike that would be forever cherished. The youngster beamed with pride when we congratulated him on his buck.

Once the sun was up, Mark suggested we hunt the timber. Deer would be bedded in heavy vegetation after feeding all night in the clearcuts.

After penetrating the forest, I felt like I was blacktail hunting in the manner I'd expected. Twenty five years ago, I'd cruised timber for the U.S. Forest Service in western Oregon. I remembered the damp, dark woods, with thick underbrush composed of wet ferns, briars, and unbelievably dense jungles that almost defied entry.

Still hunting quietly was out of the question, but I eased through the tangle of vegetation as silently as possible. At one point I jumped a buck with modest antlers, but he was gone in an instant, offering no chance for a shot.

Later in the day, Mark and I teamed up with some of his pals, making drives through heavy brush. A number of deer flushed, all of them does and fawns.

Hunters were everywhere. Many of them hunted along roads, and some put on drives. It was impossible to hunt and not see people in areas of reasonable visibility.

The next day, I hunted with Mark and his brother, Brad. The plan was to hunt clearcuts, first by watching for moving deer early in the morning, and then by glassing for bedded deer.

We hiked about a mile to the clearcut we'd hunt at first light. Brad had seen some bucks there on opening morning, but he wasn't able to get a shot at the best buck he'd spotted.

No bucks showed during our vigil, so we tried more drives. Once again we saw does and fawns, but bucks were absent. Later in the day we hunted the edges of clearcuts, areas that were shaded by the timbered borders. Still no luck.

The next day was more of the same. Mark and other local hunters blamed the lack of success on the drought. Deer were holed up in thick

I pose with my trophy blacktail. As I say, EVERY blacktail is a good blacktail.

timber, especially the bigger bucks. Rain was desperately needed, not only to improve hunting, but to end the merciless drought that left the forests parched, vulnerable to killer fires that could quickly destroy valuable timber stands.

I had a chance at a small buck the next day, but I blew it. Dan Boes had joined our group, and we decided to split up and hunt solo in second growth timber. Since the vegetation was so dense, I tried slipping along in an area that had some grassy openings.

I had just topped a ridge when I looked down and saw a deer feeding with its head down. Instantly I dropped down to the ground, propped my Winchester on my knee, and waited. The deer was only 70 yards away — a lead-pipe cinch if it was a buck.

Sure enough, I saw antlers when it raised its head. Not big antlers, mind you, but a little set of forkhorns that looked mighty good considering the terrible luck we'd been having.

When the deer dropped its head to resume feeding, I centered it in my scope and drew a fine bead. At the report of the rifle, the buck dashed off through the timber.

"Dead buck," I said to myself. "Meat on the table." I just knew he'd be lying 30 or 40 yards away.

He wasn't. I looked and looked, expecting to find him under every clump of ferns or inside every tangle of brush. There was no blood at all, but that hadn't bothered me. Plenty of deer are hit hard but leave no blood on the ground.

Presently my companions showed up. I explained the easy shot and how I was positive we'd find the deer any minute. We didn't. Not in the next minute or the next 60 minutes. I crawled through brush looking for the buck, totally mystified at the situation.

Could I have possibly missed at that close range? I couldn't believe it. Finally, after another hour of searching, my good pal Dan Boes made some uncomplimentary comments about my shooting ability. How, he wanted to know, can one miss a stationary deer at 70 yards when one has a dead rest and is shooting an accurate rifle? I told Dan that something very logical had happened, such as a minor earthquake at the moment I touched the trigger, or a defective bullet that keyholed and went wild, or something like that.

As I recall that incident, I still wonder about the shot. I always will, too. It will go down as one of life's unsolved mysteries.

My pal, Dan Boes, carries out my great big buck. It's nice being a writer and photographer. I get to take pictures of people transporting my critters.

Dan Boes and I hunted the following day. We worked our way up a mountain when I spotted five deer feeding in a hidden part of a clearcut tucked away under an old road.

One of the deer wore antlers, a small buck that hadn't yet learned the perils of feeding in the open during shooting hours. I mean a SMALL buck, with pencil-thin spikes that were barely three inches long.

I eased up to a log to rest my rifle on, and Dan whispered, "you really want that buck?"

"I want him," I replied simply.

Seconds later the buck was mine. As we worked our way over, my good pal made some comments about my questionable taste in male deer. Nonetheless, I had my first blacktail, and I was hooked for good. I was also relieved that my shooting ability hadn't gone to hell in a handcart, as they say.

These West Coast deer had aroused my curiosity and I knew I'd be back. For sure I wasn't about to say to heck with blacktail deer hunting, especially since my hard-earned buck wasn't exactly something I'd want to hang over my fireplace. Maybe I'd find his papa the next time out.

A THREE TIME LOSER IN ALABAMA

Nobody likes jinxes. They're beyond our control; we have no way of breaking them. Some jinxes hang on for a lifetime, others are finally broken through luck or persistence.

Alabama whitetails have been my biggest jinx. Despite three trips, I haven't been able to lower the boom on a buck.

The first trip was with a group of writers. We were testing some products made by an optics company, and used their scopes and binoculars during the hunt.

Unfortunately, the hunt was late in the season, after several dozen hunters had preceded us. We were hunting from blinds overlooking green fields, and most of the bucks had either been shot out or were so

I was as cold as I've ever been on a deer hunt. My warm clothes were up north.

wary they wouldn't enter the fields during shooting light.

One of the members of our group, the president of the optics company, was the only one who connected. He got a tiny spike, and was mighty proud of it. I didn't blame him.

The next hunt was supposed to be a surefire deal. My good buddy, John Phillips, an outdoor writer from Fairfield, Alabama, had lined up a hunt at famed Westervelt Lodge. The lodge is perhaps the best known in the south. Not only does it offer superb accommodations; it also produces some very fine bucks.

As luck would have it (bad luck, that is), a nasty arctic storm blew into Alabama. The storm broke all records for cold, and I'm not exaggerating when I say it was right at zero degrees.

I've spent all my life in the northern part of the U.S., and a great deal of time in the arctic, northern Canada, and some of the coldest spots in the country. Temperatures of 30 degrees below zero haven't been uncommon during my winters.

I can truthfully say that I can't remember being any colder than on the Westervelt hunt, but there was an easy explanation. I wasn't dressed for bitter cold, having left all my warm clothes at home. I had no idea that an Alabama winter could be so unbelievably harsh.

As it turned out, most Alabamans were unprepared for the cold snap, and many suffered in their homes that didn't have adequate heaters. The cold front, coupled by severe winds, broke many records in the South.

Despite the temperatures that had a wind chill factor of 25 or 30 below zero, John and I and another writer, Nick Sisley, opted to hunt. The lodge guides tried to talk us out of it, and were not at all happy at the prospects of us being out in that weather. They were worried. We convinced them that we wanted to just give it a try for a couple hours.

The hunt really wasn't all that difficult. As in many southern hunts, we simply sat in blinds and waited for deer to come in and feed in the adjacent green fields. Just sitting in those blinds in that ferocious wind, however, would have been an ordeal, but the blinds were enclosed, except for openings to see and shoot through.

My old buddy John saved the day for me. He had brought along a couple extra sleeping bags. Since the lodge provided linens, there wasn't any need to bring bags, but John anticipated the worst. Or so he said. Maybe the bags just happened to be in John's vehicle, but it didn't matter. Nick had enough warm clothes, and I welcomed the sleeping bag, intending to snuggle into it while out in the blind.

As we headed out of the lodge and the raging arctic wind hit us, the guides once again suggested we give it up until the storm passed. We weren't having it, and decided to give it a try.

We approached my blind, and the guide said, "You sure you want to hunt today?"

"I'm sure," I lied. "It's not that bad out."

"I'll come back for you in two hours," he said.

"Make it three," I responded, "and I'll be fine."

After a half hour, I wished I was in the warm lodge and had listened to the guide. The wind tore into the blind, which was on a tower in the middle of a huge field. Though I was in the bag, I was still half freezing to death. It was a summer bag, and didn't offer a whole lot of protection, but at least it was something.

There was no way I could watch the field. The wind ripped into every opening, and I lay on the floor of the tower, huddled tightly in the bag. Every 10 minutes or so I'd look out to see if any critters were crazy enough to be out in the weather.

At one point I saw three does run from the edge of the woods into the field. They bounced about as if the field was made of hot coals. I never saw deer act that way before. They dashed about helter skelter, dropping their heads to take a bite, only to dash off in another direction.

Suddenly a good buck showed up. He appeared from nowhere and rushed out to join the does in their strange behavior. Upon seeing the buck, I quickly tried to unshuck myself from the bag. By the time I got the job done, which seemed like several minutes but only took 10 seconds or so, the buck was back in the woods. I don't believe he saw or smelled me; I think he just wanted out of that treacherous wind.

He stood in the brush looking out, and I had a clear view of his chest. Under any other conditions, I would have taken a shot. He was 300 yards away, and I had a solid rest, but I knew the wind drift at that range would be terrible. I passed up the shot, and watched the white tail wave twice at me as the buck turned and raced into the thicket.

The guide returned sooner than he said, and I wasn't complaining. All the deer had disappeared by then, and I was ready to say to heck with deer hunting for the day.

"You okay?" the guide asked.

"Other than being on the verge of freezing to death, I think I'm all right," I answered, "but the next time I come to Alabama in January, I'll pack the same clothes that I'd take to the Yukon."

The guide smiled, and turned up the heater in the truck. It was good to be in that warm cab.

It happened to be Super Bowl Sunday. It was the first Super Bowl game I ever missed, because the TV in the lodge didn't pick up the channel. My brain was probably too numb from the cold to have been interested in the game, anyway.

The cold snap lingered, and we left without our bucks, though I'm sure I could have scored if the weather was with us.

A Westervelt Lodge official shows John Phillips what one of their big bucks look like. Unfortunately, we didn't see any, thanks to the arctic storm.

My next Alabama deer hunt was also with John Phillips. As usual, John had some big plan figured out. On this hunt, we'd also hunt wild boars with muzzleloader handguns. John had a black powder firearms company ship him two guns; all we had to do was figure out how to shoot them, practice until we could hit what we were aiming at, and go shoot a couple boars. There was, however, a little matter of being accompanied by a TV crew. They wanted to film our big bad wild boar hunt for an outdoor show. Before hunting pigs, we'd try deer first with rifles, and then attempt to take a boar or two.

The deer hunting wasn't too great where we hunted, so we turned our attention to the boars.

The guns we used were six-shot revolvers. You simply load each cylinder, cock the hammer, and pull the trigger. We loaded only five cylinders for safety reasons. The hammer always rested on an open cylinder.

I had the first opportunity. When our little dog bayed a boar, I moved up close and shot at what I thought was the pig. It wasn't. The boar was there, all right, but I'd shot at a black stump two inches away from the black pig.

Later, John had a chance at a running boar. Ordinarily he wouldn't have tried a shot at the rapidly moving target, but the animal was close — about 7 yards away. John's first shot hit the pig, but it was too high and the boar kept going. John fired again, hitting the boar once more, but the pig continued running.

Now John was tearing after the boar, and he was staying up with it pretty good until John tripped. He fell hard to the ground and the boar spun instantly and charged straight for John who was lying squarely on the ground.

I couldn't believe this was happening. I was standing 30 yards away with the TV show host, watching the drama unfold. You often hear about dangerous boars, but I was never overly impressed. Now this pig was on the attack, as serious as he could be.

John aimed at the charging animal and fired. The pig staggered but kept coming. John fired again; still the boar came. John's last shot was at six feet, and this time his round ball stopped the boar cold, killing it instantly.

It was an unbelievable episode. I've known John for a dozen years, and for the first time saw him at a loss for words. I don't know about him, but I was a nervous wreck after it was over and done with.

I went home without a boar, and I didn't get a deer, either. One of these days I'm going back. I'm about due to break the Alabama jinx. As far as the boars go, I can easily say to heck with them, though.

WHEN A JAIL NEVER LOOKED SO GOOD

You young men oughtta be ashamed of your self!

When I attended forestry school in Utah, my roommates and I were bound and determined to improve our menu considerably. Since we spent most of what little extra money we had on beer and girls, our meals basically consisted of ducks, rabbits, and whatever other critters we could hunt in the fall, but it was mostly ducks for dinner.

Six of us foresters lived in a house off-campus, and it was a big point of interest to make a palatable meal with what was in the freezer. There are only so many ways you can cook a damned duck. You reach a point where desperation, followed by starvation, becomes a reality. (Actually, I love to hunt ducks and to eat ducks, but when you cook them every way under the sun and you must eat ducks every night for 10 weeks in a row, something in your brain gradually makes you a little crazy and you begin to be repulsed by the sight, smell, and taste of a duck, any duck, whether it's a big, fat greenhead that just soared in from

Canada, or a redhead or canvasback that is supposed to be the Duck of all Ducks on the table. We had a good reason to say to heck with duck meat for a while.)

To add to our meat locker, we decided to go on a big deer hunt and come home with all the animals we could legally get. To achieve that objective, we borrowed a homemade trailer from one of our forestry professors. He was a great guy, a Texan, and lamented the fact that he couldn't go with us.

One of my roommates with a big pile of ducks we'd collected. They got to be extremely monotonous on the dinner table.

Since my 1956 Dodge four-door sedan was the only vehicle we owned that would make the 200-mile one-way trip to the spot we intended to hunt, we hitched the trailer to it and headed out. Our hunt area was the Ute Indian Reservation near Duchesne, Utah, a place that held lots of deer, and, at that time, offered an extra doe to hunters as well as a buck. (Soon after that hunt, which, as I recall, was in 1961, the reservation was closed to hunting by non-tribal members. It hasn't been open since.)

We didn't know precisely where we were supposed to hunt. None of us had been there before, but we had a map that showed us where to camp and hunt. Being all-knowing and infallible future forest rangers, we of course had no doubts that we could find the place.

We were wrong. We arrived in the black of night and drove all over the reservation on the worst dirt roads this side of Siberia. It wouldn't have been quite so bad if we had a rugged four-wheel drive vehicle, especially since we had to tow a trailer, but we didn't. My poor Dodge would never be the same.

Our spirits were lifted when we saw a giant buck in the headlights next to the road. That did it; we would quit looking for the X that was marked on the map. We'd camp right there and look for the buck in the morning.

We finally managed to put up a couple tents with the aid of flashlights, and we turned in around midnight. All we had on our minds was venison, sweet, delicious venison that would be a wonderful welcome to our boring, monotonous, maddening duck dinners.

We were so enthused about knocking off a few deer that we didn't pay much attention to the weather advisories we'd heard on the car radio while driving in. A storm was supposed to hit, a big time bad storm that could dump one to two feet of snow on most of Utah. In those days, weather forecasters were known to be a little bit off on their predictions, and we ignored the warnings. What did those weathermen know about weather anyway? They were all a bunch of BS-ers, as far as we were concerned. Only foresters could do no wrong.

There was just a skiff of snow on the ground and it was snowing lightly when we got up about 5 a.m. Just right. We'd be able to track deer all over the place. For sure we'd fill up the trailer with a ton of venison.

I hiked off toward a canyon by myself. I hadn't admitted it to my buddies, because I had a lot of pride, but I hadn't ever killed a deer yet. My whitetail efforts back east had drawn blanks, and so had a couple quickie mule deer hunts in Utah.

As I topped a knoll, I surprised a bunch of deer below me. I was so excited and shocked that I didn't pay attention to what was what. Any sex was legal, and all I could think of was venison, so I emptied my Winchester .30/.30 carbine in their direction. It was flock shooting at its best. I just shot without bothering to aim much, and kept on shooting.

I was glad I was alone. My memory of that split-second point in time 30 years ago is a bit fuzzy, but I believe I might have ejected a couple of unfired cartridges in my gallant efforts to put as much lead as possible in the air. I think the term "buck fever" would have applied nicely in that situation.

I did not hit a deer, and I don't believe I ever came close. To make sure, I walked over and looked in the snow that was rapidly beginning to accumulate. No blood, just a bunch of deer tracks.

I'd heard some shooting close by, so I walked over to investigate. I came upon my pal, who was dragging a doe back to camp. Great! We had a good start on our venison supply.

I helped him drag the doe, and when we arrived in camp, we saw an Indian warden talking to one of our companions. He was a nice guy, and politely told us that we'd better get out of the mountains. The storm was now a reality; there was no question about its severity. He strongly advised us to leave.

We took his word for it, and made a decision to camp closer to the main highway which was about 30 or 40 miles away, and hunt around it.

It was several hours before we left because one of the guys got a little turned around and he stumbled into camp about mid-afternoon. With the lone doe in the big trailer, we headed for lower elevations. We had no way of knowing it, but we were about to experience a fun little adventure.

The roads were horrible, with a foot of fresh snow piled on top. My tire chains saved us from getting hopelessly stuck, but it was all I could do to keep the car on the road. Plenty of other vehicles were in front of and behind us. We were part of hundreds of slow-moving parades that bleak afternoon in the Rockies, as tens of thousands of hunters made their way out of the hills.

It was with great relief when we hit the paved highway, U.S. 40, but the highway wasn't much better than the dirt roads. We'd decided to give up on the idea of hunting near the highway. Snow was still falling heavily and wasn't supposed to stop for another day or so. Traffic was bumper to bumper and moving about 2 miles per hour as hunters all over eastern Utah headed for home. It was impossible for snowplows to clear the highway because of the slow-moving traffic.

We had gone about 50 miles at a maddeningly slow pace and were a dozen miles from Heber, when I saw an idiot in my rear-view mirror attempting to pass a long line of cars, including me. All the traffic was heading toward Salt Lake City, which was about 55 miles away, and it was clear sailing in the opposite lane, but it was foolish to pass because there were literally hundreds of cars bumper to bumper and we were in a winding canyon. This fool had evidently become confused in the blizzard, and tried to cut back into the proper lane when he saw oncoming headlights. The problem was, he must not have seen us, because he suddenly swerved and nicely sideswiped me. I lost control immediately, and my Dodge headed over the bank, with six very terrified young men inside. We did a slow roll, landed on the tires, and there we sat. Miraculously, none of the doors opened when we rolled, and we were jammed so tightly in the car that no one bounced around. In those days, safety belts weren't even thought of yet, so we were lucky that no one was hurt.

The trailer hadn't fared so well. When we rolled, it broke loose, and it was totalled. My trunk also sprung open from the impact; our gear was all over the place.

We gathered up what we could find in the heavily falling snow, assisted by other motorists and the guy who caused the accident. His pickup was only lightly damaged, and he had insurance, which was a great relief. My Dad was not going to be very happy when he learned about the accident, but at least the car would be repaired. It wasn't quite totalled.

A wrecker arrived a half hour later. The guy who drove it seemed to be in great spirits, as business was booming, thanks to guys like me. The sheriff also arrived, and between his car and the wrecker, we got rides into Heber, the next town down the road.

When we asked the sheriff if there were any vacancies in motels, he shook his head. Because of hunters, every room was booked in town.

"I've got an idea," the affable sheriff said. "I've got a couple empty cells in the jailhouse. Warm and dry, and it won't cost you anything."

What a great idea. I'd never been in jail before, and the prospects of a warm night's sleep was mighty appealing. Everybody else thought it was a super idea, too.

We called some other pals to come pick us up in the morning, and were shown to our cells. I noted with satisfaction that the good sheriff kept the doors wide open. This, I figured, was the only way to spend a night in jail. As I lay there on my cot, I thought about all the other people who lived in that cage, but with the door locked.

My '56 Dodge sedan and borrowed trailer before the accident.

To heck with that, I thought, and to heck with ignoring weather forecasters. From now on I'd pay attention.

I went to sleep thinking about the doe my buddy had killed. At least we'd have a little variety in our menu, but I wasn't looking forward to telling my Dad about the car and the Professor about his trailer. Such was the life of a hunter, I concluded, and I couldn't wait to tell the girls back up on campus about our night in jail. Then I rolled over and fell asleep.

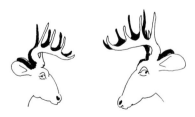

THE BIGGEST WHITETAIL OF ALL

When you think about western deer, muleys almost always come to mind. Mule deer are present in every western state, and are certainly the predominant deer species. Nonetheless, whitetails are equally at home in the west, and in some states, occur in amazing numbers. Only two western states, Utah and Nevada, have exclusively muleys, and I'm told that California may have a very small population of whitetails, otherwise it's essentially 100 percent inhabited by several subspecies of mule deer.

Of the 11 western states, no other compares with Montana for sheer numbers of whitetails. They live throughout all of the state, with the exception of some of the sagebrush country and the high mountain areas of the southwest. Biologists estimate that there may be as many whitetails as muleys; probably more.

Two Montana whitetail hunts come to mind, one in the extreme eastern region near North Dakota; the other in central Montana north of

Billings.

The first hunt was with outfitter Rocky Niles, a farmer who loved to hunt big game. When the hunting seasons approached, Rocky quit farming and guided whitetail hunters around his spread near the Missouri River. Later he took a couple hardy elk hunters and backpacked with llamas in the western mountains.

I became acquainted with Rocky through Chester Frystack, a Pennsylvania dairy farmer who loved to hunt western whitetails.

When Chester first told me about the big bucks that Rocky hunted, he got my full attention. It didn't take me long to agree to go on a hunt with Rocky.

Our party consisted of six hunters, including Chester. We hunted four ways: from treestands, driving, still hunting, and via a boat along the Missouri River. The boat got us out to brushy islands out in the river, many of which were loaded with whitetails.

We put on a drive the first day, along a wooded section adjacent to a large cultivated field. Whitetails bounced out of cover everywhere, but none were interesting enough to shoot.

Chester Frystack and his dandy Montana whitetail. He swore he wouldn't shoot one on the first day, but this buck changed his mind.

At one point we spread out and walked through the woods, each of us walking about 100 yards apart. I came to a small patch of brush about twice as big as my pickup truck, and was about to walk around it when something made me stop. I didn't see or hear anything, but I picked up a hefty branch and tossed it into the brush pile.

A buck exploded from within, and bounded away toward Chester, who was walking adjacent to me. I didn't have a good shot at the fleeing buck, and I didn't want to shoot because I wasn't sure where Chester was, but I saw enough to know it was a dandy buck.

I didn't really expect Chester to shoot, because he swore up and down that he was going to hold out for a trophy. He was no stranger to big whitetails, and had collected several from Montana, Alberta, and other places.

That's why I was surprised when Chester shot. I walked over and saw him standing over the buck, a fine animal carrying a nine-point rack.

"I'm pleased with him," Chester said with a big grin, "but I wish I'd waited. There are bigger bucks around here."

"Why'd you shoot," someone asked.

"This son-of-a-gun was steaming along right toward me," Chester exclaimed. "All I saw was a good set of antlers as the buck bore down on me. He looked twice as big as he does now."

Though Chester wanted a bigger buck, he graciously accepted the one he killed. Chester earned my respect by doing so. I don't care much for people who weigh their hunting success solely on the size of the animal they shoot. In my opinion, there's much more to hunting than what grows on a critter's head. To be sure, I've passed up lots of animals over the years, looking for the big one, but I've never been mad because I didn't get anything or got a lesser animal than I'd anticipated.

After Chester's buck was field dressed and moved into the shade, we continued our walk. I saw five more bucks, but all were fairly small. One had an eight point rack, but he had a narrow spread and short tines.

The next day we headed for the river. We'd walk the river bottoms, and at one spot we'd use a boat, and hunt weedy islands.

Deer were numerous, but so were pheasants. Big gaudy roosters exploded from cover everywhere. I was amazed, and eager to hunt them. Rocky informed us that if we'd hurry up and get our bucks, we could trade our rifles for shotguns and hunt pheasants. That sounded like a great plan to me. I love to hunt birds, but do very little of it anymore because I seem to spend most of my time in the mountain country hunting big game.

The islands held more pheasants and plenty of deer, too. Whitetails gave us the slip here and there by swimming the river and evaporating into cover on the mainland.

No one did any good, so later that afternoon we hunted another area. Two hunters scored, one of them an elderly gentleman who had trouble getting around. He was from the east, and his son told us that this might be one of his Dad's final hunts. We were delighted that the older man got his buck.

Just before dark, Chester and I were riding with Rocky in his pickup, generally looking the country over. We still had four days to hunt, and Chester had been taking lots of good-natured kidding because he shot the first buck he saw. Throughout the day, his pals reminded him that he had intended to hold out to the bitter end for a monster buck.

That's why Chester got a little bit sick when we gazed at the giant buck in the field along the road. In all my years of hunting, I'd never seen a bigger whitetail. Neither had Chester.

This buck had a high, wide, massive rack, with long tines. He was an absolutely outstanding animal.

"My Lord, that buck will make the Boone and Crockett record book," Chester moaned as we glassed the deer with binoculars. "What an animal."

"Think you can hit him from here?" Rocky asked me. "The buck is on my property."

I didn't answer right off, because I was weighing all the factors. The range was about 375 yards, maybe 400, and the wind was blowing — not very strong, but enough to cause significant wind drift in the bullet. The buck was staring at us, and was about 10 feet from the edge of cover adjacent to the field. About 30 does and fawns were near him, and none of the animals appeared spooked by our presence. If I elected to try a shot, I could easily slip up to a sturdy fencepost 10 yards away and get a solid rest for my rifle.

"I'll walk up to the fence and see how it feels," I told Rocky. "He's a long way off and I don't like the way the wind is blowing."

I eased up to the fence, and looked at the buck through my scope. He was still watching me, and I felt like I had a good solid rest. I had confidence in my ability to hit him in the vitals. The fence rest was exceptionally comfortable, and the wind had suddenly been reduced to a mild breeze. I was used to long range shooting, having done it for many years at antelope, elk, muleys, sheep, and other big game species. The biggest whitetail I'd ever seen in my life was now at my mercy. I raised the rifle a touch; the dot reticle settled over the top of his back just where I wanted it.

Suddenly I had the feeling that something wasn't quite right. The idea of shooting this giant buck a few yards from the truck bothered me.

I shot this buck from a treestand the day after I saw the giant. I was nonetheless satisfied with this deer.

Sure, I've taken my share of animals that I'd spotted from a road, but something was different about this buck. It didn't seem fair to shoot him this way. He was too majestic, too much of an exquisitely beautiful animal to be shot from alongside a road. Maybe another time I'd have taken the shot, but at that moment I hesitated.

My brain rationalized that the buck didn't seem to be disturbed by us, and he'd probably be in the same area in the morning. There was a good chance I'd see him again.

Rocky slipped up to me. "I think I'll pass," I whispered. "Too far.

Can we hunt him in the morning?"

"I have treestands all through those woods," Rocky said. "We'll hunt him tomorrow."

As we walked the few yards to the truck, the buck suddenly ran to the edge of the field and jumped into the woods, stopping to stare at us from the cover. That's how we left him as we drove away.

While driving to Rocky's house, I realized that someone else could kill the buck in the morning. He wasn't exclusively mine; I expected Rocky would put all the hunters in the treestands, but it was my choice to let the buck go. No use regretting it.

I was in my treestand long before sunup. As shooting light appeared, I honestly saw 100 deer in the fields. My stand was situated close enough to the field where I could see out. Several bucks were evident, but I didn't see the giant, though he could have been just out of sight.

The plan was for Rocky and his guide to drive deer toward us in the treestands as soon as the animals started leaving the field for bedding areas.

The strategy worked well. Dozens of deer were streaming through the woods toward me. I looked them over as fast as I could, because they were moving at a good clip, though they stopped every now and then to look around.

About 50 deer went by me, but the big buck wasn't with them. My heart sank as I saw Rocky heading toward me, indicating the drive was over. Moments later two bucks ran toward my treestand. One looked to have a high rack, and I made a quick decision to take him. I had the distinct feeling that the monster was long gone.

I shot, and the buck dropped to the forest floor. He was a nice 9-pointer, but far from being the buck that the big boy was. I was tickled, though, and besides, now I had the rest of the time to hunt pheasants. At least, that was my way of justifying the shot. I got what I came for. The big one got away, which is why he was so big. That's the way it often goes in the deer woods.

The next year I hunted in north central Montana on what turned out to be the quickest whitetail hunt I'd ever been on. A friend invited me to hunt a ranch that held some very good bucks, and I made plans to hunt it about mid-season.

During the drive up from my home in Wyoming, I ran into a nasty blizzard. I'm used to rough weather, but this storm was a bad one, and

I got this nice Montana whitetail buck in a nasty blizzard. I'm glad I decided to stick out the storm instead of turning around and going home, which I almost did!

radio weather advisories said to stay off the roads.

At one point I turned my truck around and headed back home, but I only went a few miles before I changed my mind. I turned around again and headed north for Montana.

The storm was in full swing when I arrived at the ranch. At least 16 inches was piled up, and a fierce wind was whipping the powder into huge snowdrifts.

My friend suggested we take a short ride before dark to look over the ranch a bit. I brought along my rifle, just in case something interesting showed up.

We'd only driven a mile when we spotted a bunch of deer in a pocket of willows next to a field. Binoculars indicated one was a buck, and he was a nice buck at that.

It was decision time. I had three days to hunt, but the blizzard was supposed to last for another day or so. My host helped me make up my mind.

"That's a great buck," he said. "A really good buck."

"Do they come much bigger than that?" I asked.

"No," he answered.

Decision time was over. I waded through knee-deep snow, took a rest on a tree, and drilled the buck through the center of the neck. And that was that. He was a fat 10-pointer with a handsome rack.

I spent the rest of the hunt taking pictures and enjoying the winter wonderland. Montana had come through again with a nice whitetail, but I'll always remember the big guy at Rocky's place. What a buck, and what memories I have of him. Good memories, even though every now and then I regret not shooting him. But when I think about that precise moment, about how I felt, I know I made the right decision. Maybe another day I'll see a giant buck, and if I'm near a road, and if he's on property I can hunt, and if I can get a legal shot, I might just say to heck with passing him up.

We'll see.

TREESTANDS ARE FOR THE BIRDS

Y···· ER···· YEA···· Looks good'T ME!

I hate treestands. I dislike being up in the air, trusting a few boards, branches, nails, or wire. I don't much care for being blasted by the frigid wind, or staying in one place for hours at a time.

For practical reasons, I don't appreciate the need to limit my shooting angles to avoid being knocked out of the tree when I fire my rifle. In some treestands I've been in, it was physically impossible to swivel around and take a shot at a buck approaching from behind me.

I know — many treestands are perfectly safe, especially when you use a belt or a rope that will hold you securely if something under you breaks. I don't mind heights or being in trees. In fact, for years I owned a part-time tree removal business in which I had to scamper across branches, cutting the tree down limb by limb.

But I still hate treestands.

That attitude was pestering me as Harold Knight and I walked to the Tennessee hollow in the predawn darkness. Harold had located some fresh primary scrapes and was excited about what the morning would bring. He had erected a treestand near the scrape he wanted me to watch.

It was opening morning, and we were both anxious for shooting light. But I wasn't looking forward to the confounded treestand.

"What do you think of it?" Harold whispered as I peered up at the contraption in the poor gray light.

"Looks nice," I lied, "but I'm not much of a treestand person."

"Try it out," Harold suggested.

I knew what my opinion would be before I climbed, but I climbed anyway.

"Very comfortable," I lied again. "Not bad at all."

"Good," Harold said politely as he helped me get my rifle up the tree. "I figured you'd like it."

Then he pointed in the general direction of the scrape and applied some scent in the area. Because I had been invited on this hunt by some folks who market a deer scent, we naturally used their product. That was logical, but it was going to be an interesting experience for me. I hadn't used scents much and had no strong opinions regarding their effectiveness.

The stand creaked as a breeze came up and swayed the hickories and oaks, especially the oak in which I was sitting. I was relieved when Harold finally disappeared, because I came down out of the tree with a swiftness that would have put a chimp to shame.

I reasoned that the steep hillside behind me would serve very nicely as a vantage point. It was good to have terra firma under my boots.

As daylight crept into the woods, I acquainted myself with the surroundings. The scrape Harold had located was on a slight knoll next to an old woods road. I couldn't see the scrape from my position, but it was in a typical spot.

Above the scrape, a thick stand of pines formed a dense thicket, a perfect spot to harbor a sneaking buck. Behind me, a patch of dense laurels covered the slope, creating another avenue of approach for a buck intent on checking his scrapes.

I felt comfortable in those Tennessee woods. Though I'm a Yankee, the oak/hickory forest looked exactly like the countryside I had hunted in my home state of New York. I'd been living in the Rockies for more than two decades, and the Southern woods brought back nostalgic memories.

As I waited for something to happen, I slapped at an annoying mosquito and was amazed by its presence in mid-November. I couldn't help but think of several of the cold weather hunts in the Rockies that I'd already been on that season. Mosquitos were history months ago.

The Tennessee woods were strangely silent except for a few distant crows and an occasional blue jay. I hadn't seen a deer, and I was getting the urge to move around and stillhunt. My vigil at the scrape was more than two hours old, and the sun was shining brightly. I was convinced

I'm mighty happy with this Tennessee whitetail. Didn't need to sit in the treestand, either.

that the deer would be bedded. The temperature was around 60 degrees, and there were no hunters in the vicinity to push the whitetails around.

Harold and I agreed to meet at the truck at 10 a.m., and it was just about time to go when I heard something running toward me in the laurel thicket. The footfalls sounded like a deer moving along briskly, but I couldn't be positive.

The disturbance was directly behind me, so I eased around and leaned my back against a tree where I could raise my rifle easily. If a buck showed, the shot would be close, no more than 25 yards.

Finally, an animal moved into view. It was indeed a deer, and I

Harold Knight checks out the hot scrape that apparently attracted my buck.

slowly inched my rifle up toward my shoulder.

What I saw next made me gasp. A big rack materialized on the animal's head, and it took me only a second to locate his chest in the laurels. He had his nose to the ground and was weaving through the brush at a very fast walk.

My scope was full of deer when I squeezed the trigger. The buck collapsed at the shot as my .30/06 Remington Core-Lokt bullet took him through both lungs.

I couldn't believe it when I walked up to him. The buck had 10 points, long tines and an almost perfectly symmetrical rack with a 20-

inch spread.

I don't know what the deer was doing on that balmy day. He seemed to be heading straight for the scrape, but I interrupted him on his route. I like to think that he was doing everything he should have been doing during the rut — heading for an active scrape and perhaps reacting to the odor of the scent that Harold had applied.

I field dressed the buck and headed for the meeting spot with Harold. He didn't quite believe my account of the size of the buck and was delighted when he saw it. The buck wasn't even close to record size, but evidently it was outstanding for that part of the state.

At the time we hunted, Tennessee law allowed you to take five bucks, but you had to validate each buck at a check station before you could get another. When we brought my buck in, the wildlife officers on duty were impressed. They said it was the biggest buck to come out of the county in a year or two.

I was impressed, too. I'm not much of a trophy hunter; I usually settle for a representative animal. It was nice to take something well over the average animal.

I often wonder if I could have gotten a shot at the buck from the treestand. He came in close and fast, and from the opposite direction of where I was watching. I like to think the treestand might have cost me the buck. For sure, I've still said to heck with them, using them only out of respect when I hunt with fine hosts like Harold.

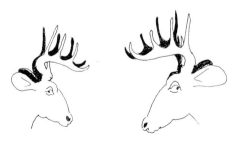

A couple of whitetail bucks at ease in the woods.

HOW MANY POINTS DID THOSE BUCKS HAVE?

The three big muley bucks boiled over the ridgetop and bounded down the steep slope into the sagebrush flat. As soon as they reached the bottom, they suddenly stopped, looked around a bit, and began cautiously feeding. They were as nervous as muleys can get. Just before they appeared, I heard a single shot over the top of the ridge that they were rapidly departing from.

I lay in the sagebrush with my son, Danny, who was about 12 years old at the time. The trio of bucks would soon be in for a rude surprise. One of them was about to be a big part of my winter's food supply.

I glassed the deer with my binoculars, intending to evaluate them, pick out the best of the bunch, and drop him in his tracks. The animals were only 125 yards out, the wind was perfect, I had a solid rest, and the bucks had no idea I was so close to their world. It was a perfect setup, and I was already tasting venison stew as I glassed them over.

I was hunting in Wyoming, in my favorite part of the state. I was a nonresident at the time, living in Utah to the south. The bucks were about what I expected in Wyoming. They were dandies, with deep chests, bodies rolling with muscle and fat, and their antlers were heavy and wide. The region I hunted was fairly tough to draw a tag in, and when I did I figured it would be no problem to take a great muley. A restriction in my hunting unit required legal bucks to have at least four points on one side. I was sure I'd see a four-pointer on the mountain I hunted.

The year before I applied for the unit, I hunted it for sage grouse. I saw so many big bucks while bird hunting that I quickly decided to try for a tag there the following fall. After successfully getting the tag, I again hunted grouse in it a couple months before deer season. The big bucks were still there.

Now, while watching the three bucks in the sage, I knew I'd made a good choice. Deer season in Wyoming would be over for me in a few seconds.

I carefully scanned the first buck with my binoculars. Not legal. He had a beautiful 30-inch wide rack, but only three points on each side. I looked at the next buck. He too was a big animal, with a set of antlers about 28 inches wide and very high. He wasn't legal, either. Like the first, he was also a three-pointer. Surely the third buck would have four points on one antler. Three point bucks this big weren't common; seeing a trio of them in a bunch would be a rare event.

I couldn't believe my eyes when the third buck had only three points, just as the first two. It was impossible. Three big, fat, mature bucks, and none had four points on one antler.

Deciding that one of the deer surely had a small but legal fourth point that I hadn't seen, I settled into the sage, propped my binoculars up to a steady position, and intently scrutinized the deer. As I glassed them they continued to feed in the sagebrush, and hadn't moved 10 yards from where they initially stopped.

I took the racks apart with my eyes, chunk by chunk. The binoculars targeted in on the base of each antler, then slowly followed it to its first fork, and then to the end of the beam which formed the third point. I did that six times, and six times I came up short. It was truly impossible. Each buck indeed wore three points to the side.

Suddenly one of the bucks bedded down before our eyes. Presently the other two did the same. As they lay there, chewing their cuds, I looked them over again. Still no fourth point in sight.

Danny and I were in a good position. A clump of serviceberry bushes concealed us from the deer. Unless the wind changed, we weren't likely to be spotted, but there wasn't much reason to hide any longer. It was time to move on, to look for a legal buck.

We could have slipped away unseen, but I decided to look over the deer one last time. I hadn't gotten a good look at the back side of every antler; perhaps there was a freak tine sticking out at an odd angle.

Wyoming law required a legal point to be long enough to be able to hang a ring on it.

In order to see the back sides of the antlers, there was only one way to do it. I jumped up and shouted, and the bucks were instantly on their feet. As they ran, I looked at a blur of antlers as closely as I could — still no fourth point.

Danny and I hiked back toward the truck, slowly glassing and still hunting as we moved along. We were eating lunch at the truck when a game warden pulled up and walked over.

"Any luck?" he asked.

"Not yet," I responded. "We haven't seen a legal buck yet."

"Did you see any bucks?" he questioned.

"Three," I answered, "and they were dandies, but every one of them was a three-pointer."

The game warden seemed surprised. "You mean none of them had brow tines?" the warden said. "In Wyoming, they count, too."

I couldn't believe it. Brow tines! Every buck had brow tines, but I hadn't considered them as being legal points. In Utah, where I hunted most, brow tines didn't count. But this wasn't Utah — it was Wyoming, and I'd made a dumb mistake.

The warden knew I was not happy with myself, politely checked my tag, and left. He advised me about a couple places that might offer pretty good bucks.

As soon as he drove away, I read the deer regulations. Sure enough, brow tines counted.

I cussed some, but not as much as I would have if my young son wasn't with me. Besides, there were plenty more bucks out there, and it was only the first day of the season.

We drove up over the ridgetop where the bucks had run down from, and I saw a bunch of magpies feeding on a gut pile. Obviously the single shot I'd heard that morning was on target. What was interesting was the fact that it appeared that the buck that was shot was no doubt with the trio. Why then, did those three bucks calm down immediately after they hit the sagebrush bottom? You'd think they'd have run out of the county. They should have been plenty spooked.

Danny and I hiked around the mountains for the rest of the weekend, and left for home Sunday night. I'd seen lots of deer, including some small four-point bucks, but I decided to pass. None were as big as the so-called three pointers we'd seen, and I made a decision to wait until a right big buck came by.

I couldn't get back to Wyoming until a week later. This time I took Janette, my 13-year old daughter, and we hunted another unit. In Wyoming, nonresidents can draw a tag for only one of about a dozen regions. Each region is composed of many units, each with separate restrictions and hunting seasons.

The unit I hunted with Janette was desert country with rocky outcrops erupting high out of the desert floor. A pal of mine who worked for the BLM in Wyoming told me there were some huge bucks in those rocky ridges. Furthermore, any buck was legal in the unit, but I was still holding out for a big guy.

It was unseasonably warm when we hiked those steep hills, and I was glad we'd brought a canteen of water. Our efforts were in vain, however. We hadn't seen a single buck, though I glassed all the good looking spots, as well as the bad looking spots, too, and we hiked into all the hidden recesses and pockets that might hold a buck.

We went home without seeing even a doe, and my pal told me later that the water holes had completely dried up and the deer had moved out. Such was hunting — at least I'd lost a few pounds during the strenuous climbing.

The last day of the season was equally uneventful, though I'd seen a number of small bucks. A couple of them had 24-inch spreads that I would have welcomed another time, but I was going to wait it out. I had a tag in Utah, and wasn't worried about getting a buck there. During the Wyoming hunt it would be a big buck or nothing.

It ended up being nothing, but I thoroughly enjoyed the hunt. I've always figured that you don't have to kill something to have a successful hunting trip. After the hunt, I was even able to smile about the trio of big bucks that had the last laugh. I still smile when I think about that day, which is the way it should be. I believe that hunting memories, even those of failed hunts, should be accepted as part of the total experience.

The next time I hunt a unit with an antler restriction, however, you can bet your boots that I'll know the law inside and out. To heck with being ignorant of the regulations!

WHEN THE WEATHERBY BIT ME IN TEXAS

I 'd always wanted to hunt desert mule deer, and when my good pal Murry Burnham invited me to hunt them on his ranch in south Texas, I immediately took him up on it. Besides muleys, Murry had some decent whitetails, as well as a bunch of javelina. As an extra bonus, big catfish lived in the Rio Grande River that bordered his ranch to the south. The property was near Del Rio on the Mexican border, about as far south as you can get in Texas.

Rick Schroeder, the young actor who played in many TV sit-coms, movies, and TV feature shows, was also in our party. He had met Murry when he was shooting the movie "Lonesome Dove", at a nearby ranch several months prior to hunting season. Rick hunted both ranches, and the timing was just right for him to be at Murry's when I was there.

I didn't know what to expect of Rick, but he turned out to be a very polite, well-mannered young man. I suppose I'd anticipated a spoiled brat from Hollywood, but I was pleasantly surprised. Another unexpected aspect was Rick's hunting ability. He was skilled at spotting game, stalking, shooting, and was well versed in deer behavior.

On the first morning of the hunt, Rick, Murry and I hiked about in the hills, and saw a number of desert muleys, but we passed on the bucks. About mid-morning we split up, Rick and Murry going off in one direction; me in another.

It was nearing noon when I topped a rise and spotted a nice buck. He was across a draw, and about 150 yards away. I couldn't take a kneeling position because of high cactus around me, so I got into my sling, snugged the rifle up tight, and drew a bead on the buck.

I pose with my desert muley, and I have a Band-Aid over my nose to prove my scope wound.

What happened next was not exactly what I had in mind. Because I was leaning over a high cactus and shooting at an awkward angle, and because I was using my .300 Weatherby Mag, the recoil of the rifle belted me nicely. I mean a really good jolt.

The scope dug deeply into my eyebrow, and my contact lens flipped out of my eye and onto my lower eyelid. I was blind and bleeding, but my pride was hurt more than my head.

After a lifetime of hunting, I'd never been bitten by a scope, but I predicted it would happen, and in fact I predicted it in my mule deer book written in 1980. There was a humorous side to the incident, however. The Weatherby had been given to me by General Chuck Yeager during an elk hunt in British Columbia two years prior to the Texas hunt. The rifle scope bit him on that hunt, and we made light of the situation. Now the tables were turned, and the joke was on me.

I stumbled to camp, with the contact in my mouth to keep it moist, and my tee shirt pressed over my eye to control the bleeding. I wasn't looking forward to the reception I'd get, but I deserved it.

Rick and Murry were in camp making lunch, and when they took a look at me they were kind; in fact they were worried. My contact wasn't damaged, and a Band-Aid fixed the cut. In a few minutes I was back in shape and ready to hunt again.

That afternoon, Murry and I headed out on the ranch while Rick hunted solo. We spotted a good muley, not huge as muleys go, but a nice buck for that part of the world. A drop-tine on each antler made him a nontypical.

This time I held the Weatherby correctly and the buck was mine at the shot. He was my first desert muley, and I was pleased.

That evening we planned to hunt varmints. We'd try predator calling, using Murry's special night light. Murry drove his old two-seater jeep. I sat in the passenger seat, and Rick stood on the tailgate. As we headed out the gate in the dark, Rick let out a yelp and jumped off the jeep. An unseen wire that was stretched across the gate caught him at eye level, and he suffered a cut about as bad as mine. We gave up the varmint hunt, tended to his wound, and spent the rest of the evening telling hunting tales.

Rick left for the other ranch the next morning, and I took a hike to an area known to have plenty of javelina. Sure enough, the little pigs were there, and I collected my limit of two, using Murry's .308. I intended to cook the javelina, and didn't want to mess them up any more than was necessary. The Weatherby would definitely have messed them up.

Later I drove to the airport to pick up Vin Sparano, who was Executive Editor of *OUTDOOR LIFE* (Vin is now Editor-in-chief). We began hunting deer immediately, and I managed to take a fairly decent whitetail buck.

That afternoon, we drove down to the Rio Grande River, where Murry set Vin up in a blind. My deer hunting was over, so Murry and

Rick Shroeder and I point to our battle scars from our Texas deer hunt.

I went catfishing while Vin waited for a deer.

The walk along the river was most interesting. Very thick cane grew in clumps that were so tight and dark within that you couldn't see a thing. Tunnels and pathways formed a maze in the cane, and in that maze was a wild bull or two that had swam the river from the Mexico side onto Murry's ranch. The bulls were of the very mean variety, and would attack with the least provocation. Murry said they'd attack with NO provocation, which made the fishing rods in our hands seem a mite useless. We walked gingerly through the cane, looking and listening for a nasty brute that would weigh close to a ton or better. I had my eye on a stout tree every now and then along our route, just in case I needed to climb one in a hurry.

No bulls showed up, we caught some big catfish, and Vin killed a nice buck from the stand.

Vin got another deer the next day, and I pulled a neat trick when I was ready to leave camp for the airport. The plan was for Vin to go with Murry to the ranch that Rick had gone to, but I fouled up our departure a bit by locking the keys to my rental car inside the car. The windows were closed tightly, of course, and in my efforts to pry open a back window, it completely shattered. I managed to retrieve the keys, and left Vin and Murry to complete the hunt. As it turned out, Vin killed a nice buck on the other ranch, and every one went home happy.

That's the way every hunt should be, but I could have lived without getting the Weatherby scar. On the bright side, I knew it was going to happen once, but I said to heck with it ever happening again — at least when there's a movie star in camp.

Dewey was not happy with me when I shot the buck down in the canyon.

PLEASE DON'T SHOOT A DEER DOWN THERE

It was in the mid-70's when an old pal invited me to hunt elk, deer, and birds with him in a game-rich area of Idaho. My buddy, Dewey Haeder, was a college classmate back in the 60's. We'd attended forestry school together at Utah State, and managed to sneak away from campus quite frequently to hunt and fish whatever was in season.

After college, Dewey went to work for the U.S. Forest Service, as did many of my pals. Dewey was based in Grangeville, Idaho, working on the Nez Perce National Forest when we made the hunt.

The plan was to try first for elk, than muleys, and then chukars and Hungarian partridge. We'd hunt birds if we had time, and I'll admit I was anxious because the area around Grangeville teemed with upland game birds.

The elk hunt wasn't exactly a ripping success. We parked a camper in the forest, and immediately got off to a bad start. It seemed that another party of people believed they had rights to our camp unit, even though we were in a national forest, in a fairly remote location where there was no reserved camping. Our spot was at least 50 yards from the other party's, but they didn't care for our presence. To show their displeasure, this group of fools (I won't call them sportsmen -- they didn't deserve the name), started shooting guns off aimlessly. At the same time, they passed around a jug of whiskey, and continued to fire handguns and rifles into the air, and into the surrounding forest. Their idea, which worked very well, was to persuade us to depart from the camp area, which they evidently had intended for some friends to use.

Dewey and I weren't about to argue with a bunch of drunken idiots, so we simply drove off and camped in another campground a couple miles away. No sense asking for trouble, and those jerks with the whiskey weren't worth the effort of a confrontation, which had the makings of being mighty ugly.

While I rounded up some firewood and got dinner started, Dewey slipped away into the forest with his bow and soon returned with a trio of spruce grouse. Known as fool hens, the birds were arrowed as they sat in a tree watching Dewey.

One nice thing about fool hens — you'll always have a fresh supply of meat if you can find a couple birds. All you need is a rock or two and a good aim, or a slingshot, bow, handgun — even a long stick. When they're on the ground, you can often whack one on the noggin. If you intend to do this, be sure the state you're hunting allows you to take birds with means other than a shotgun. Some don't.

The elk hunt began early the next morning, before daybreak, and by midmorning we were busting through one of the nastiest spruce blowdowns I'd ever been in. We sounded like several herds of elephants, and, of course, no elk hung around long enough to offer a shot.

A few more days of slipping along dark creek bottoms, over ridges, and the edges of meadows were unsuccessful, so we packed up and headed out. Mule deer and birds were next on the agenda.

For muleys we hunted the lovely breaks of the Salmon River, a deep canyon with steeply sloping walls covered with cheatgrass, sagebrush, and laced with pockets of brush and trees in the damp draws. Dewey's son, Tom, went along with us on the trip.

Before we started, Dewey looked down into the vast chasm and made a profound statement. "Whatever you do," he said, "don't shoot a deer way down there. Hunt high, and remember where the truck is parked." I knew precisely what Dewey meant. The truck was parked up on the ridgetop, and it would be a very long, steep — very steep — drag up to the truck if someone was foolish enough to kill a deer low on the slopes.

I had every intention of following Dewey's sage advice, but I kept dropping lower as I hunted. For some reason, the cover looked better down below.

My brain was apparently not activated when the three-point muley bounced out of a pocket of brush. Without weighing the consequences, my finger instantly found the safety, and then the trigger, as I shouldered the Winchester. Moments later the deer was down, and a few moments after that I knew I was in trouble with my buddy.

I barely had the buck field dressed when Dewey showed up. As I expected, he was most unhappy with me, and I won't repeat his greeting upon seeing the dead deer.

Tom carried our rifles as we proceeded to drag the carcass up the nasty slope. As I tried to convince my pal, he should have been pleased that I didn't shoot a really big buck. The one we were dragging weighed only about 165 pounds, but my buddy wasn't the least impressed by my rationalization. He kept muttering nasty things about trigger-happy hunters, steep mountains, dragging deer uphill, and other related subjects.

It was a terrible drag, the worst I can ever remember. I've been in other similar situations, but on later hunts I used my brain a whole lot more than my back. It was considerably easier to cut a buck in two pieces, and drag each one, this cutting the weight you're dragging by 50 percent. There are also nifty devices and concepts these days that make dragging a whole lot easier — even uphill.

We didn't use any of those good ideas that day in Idaho. We simply each grabbed an antler and pulled, and pulled. It was all we could do to move the carcass much more than eight or ten feet each time we pulled up. We'd take a break, cuss a little, and then pull the deer another eight feet.

It was nearing dark when we approached the truck. I think maybe I

We take a break from dragging my buck. Dewey looks across the canyon at a bunch of chukars.

kissed the truck, just as I've been known to occasionally kiss a horse after a long day's hike in the mountains.

The pain was soon forgotten though, especially since the next day we had a sensational hunt for chukars and huns. I'm not exaggerating when I say we flushed 500 chukars before noon. We had our limits in no time, as Dewey's big black Lab, Barney, retrieved birds from the cheatgrass slopes. After dressing the chukars, we headed to weedy areas along stubblefields and each picked up a limit of huns.

I headed home without an elk, but with a decent buck and plenty of birds. It had been a great hunt.

An interesting incident occurred on the way home. Since I'd be driving home to Utah during the night when the temperature was cool, and my Ramcharger was packed to the gills with hunting and camping gear, I lashed the buck atop the vehicle.

It was a long drive, about 12 hours from central Idaho to northeast Utah, and I was driving through Roosevelt, Utah about 8:30 in the morning, just a short distance from Vernal, where I lived.

I was about 10 miles out of Roosevelt when I saw the flashing lights of a highway patrol vehicle behind me. I pulled over, and the policeman told me that a barber in Roosevelt had seen me go by with a deer. Since the Utah season wasn't open, the barber figured he'd made a great discovery and called the police. Evidently the barber didn't realize that other states had different seasons than Utah. At least he was doing his duty by reporting a would-be poacher, but I'd never heard of a poacher transporting an illegal animal in full view of the world.

Presently a game warden drove up, having been notified by the trooper. The warden was a hunting buddy of mine, and he had a big grin when he recognized me. The warden knew I hunted out of state a great deal, and when he checked the Idaho tag we had a good laugh.

I wasn't laughing, however, when the trooper glanced at my license plates and informed me that they'd expired the week before. In my haste to prepare for the hunt, I forgot about getting new plates. I ended up parting with $50 to pay the fine, and the barber had the last laugh after all.

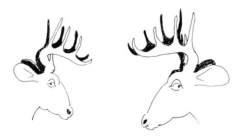

Not the biggest blacktail in Washington, but good enough for me. He was great eating!

A TALE OF A DUMB BLACKTAIL

A couple years ago, I was invited to hunt blacktail deer and Roosevelt elk in western Washington. Bert Day, who was involved with the Rocky Mountain Elk Foundation Chapter in Vancouver, Washington, asked if I'd agree to accompany the highest bidder on an auctioned hunt. That person would hunt with me and Garry Day, Bert's husband. Bert would do the cooking, and we'd stay at her and Garry's camp near Cougar, Washington. We would hunt on the Gifford Pinchot National Forest that became instantly famous when Mt. St. Helens blew its top in 1981. Much of the forest was devastated in the blast, but I'd be hunting in the area that was untouched by the eruption.

My hunting partners included Garry Day and Ray Croswell, from Vancouver, Washington, and Carl Phillips, who was high bidder.

Elk were our initial quarry, but blacktails were also on the list. I was eager to take a good blacktail. This was my second hunt for them; the first had resulted in a small spike. A severe drought had plagued us on that first hunt, but we wouldn't be having that kind of weather situation in the Mt. St. Helens area. Five inches poured down on us opening day, and I re-established my fondness for wool. Garry, Carl, and I hunted in vain for elk while Ray checked out an area that offered a late deer hunt.

A second day of nonstop rain was equally uneventful. We decided to move our base of operations to another part of the Gifford Pinchot

If you like to hunt in the rain, head for western Washington or Oregon. You probably won't be let down.

Forest where both deer and elk were legal quarry. Only elk were allowed in the initial unit we hunted.

Ray suggested that Garry and I hunt a timbered mountain slope laced with openings occupied by scrub oak, while he and Carl hunted a similar area. According to Ray, blacktails favored the slope, feeding on acorns and brush.

The incessant rains had finally let up, and a bit of sunshine poked through leaden clouds. The oaks seemed to be wearing jewels as raindrops glistened from soggy leaves, but the rain soon began again, this time more lightly but with determined persistence.

Garry and I split up, slowly still hunting the oak patches. I had good vibes about this area. Sign was plentiful and the place seemed to scream bucks, but the furtive deer again proved to be uncooperative. I was beginning to think I was hunting whitetails in disguise. The next day we tried another spot, and lucked into some fresh elk sign. Garry and I got into a herd of about 20 elk in thick timber just as shooting hours were about to end, but we couldn't sort out bulls in the heavy underbrush. So much for the elk.

Ray had initially told us that he was exclusively interested in deer, so he was all excuses and apologies the next morning when he downed a fat four-point bull elk. Garry, Carl, and I were not sympathetic as we backpacked the quarters of Ray's elk off the mountain. Ray complained that some guys couldn't take a joke.

The next year, 1989, I was back hunting with Garry and Ray in the same spot we'd hunted the year previous. I was more determined than ever to take a blacktail buck.

Garry had scouted the area for three days prior to the season and had located several bucks, all of them feeding in clearcuts. The weather was unsettled, with intermittent rain and broken clouds.

On opening morning I headed for the timber, hoping to find a blacktail in the forest that had been so frustrating to hunt. I was learning that blacktails are like ghosts in the heavy forest. They were tough critters, as tough to find as any big game species I'd ever hunted. I wasn't anxious to hunt clearcuts with the crowds of hunters that I knew would be about.

Opening day was a blank. I saw a few does and fawns, but nothing that carried antlers.

Garry suggested I try a clearcut the next day that required a two mile walk from the main road. A locked gate precluded vehicle access, and Garry was certain that few, if any hunters would walk that far.

I parked my truck at the gate before daybreak, and headed down the road that funneled through magnificent Douglas fir forests. By first light I slipped up to the edge of the clearcut and immediately spotted a dozen deer moving about in the brush. Two were bucks, both of them spikes that were illegal in the unit. Bucks had to be at least forked-horns or better.

Backing off from my position, I noted the wind direction and worked my way through the timber. My destination was the bottom of the clearcut a quarter mile away.

The buck was among a half-dozen deer. He wasn't a candidate for the record book, but his three points to the side immediately earned my respect and full attention.

My .270 Kimber settled onto a log and I centered him in my scope. The deer collapsed at the shot, and I saw two other legal bucks scamper away with at least 15 other deer.

The buck lay in a nasty hole, so I dressed him and covered him with brush to protect him from ravens that were already squawking overhead.

I returned the next day with a couple pals and a Pac'Orse, a nifty one-wheeled rig designed to haul game out of tough spots. The Pac'Orse, manufactured by my friend Freeman Cockram of Vancouver, Washington, turned an uphill ordeal into a snap. We had the buck to my truck in no time.

A humorous incident occurred when my two friends went with me to pack out the buck. One of them had a deer tag, and he had never taken a deer. I badly wanted him to get his first buck on this hunt.

Before approaching the clearcut on the way in, we stashed the Pac'Orse a short distance up the road and sneaked to the edge of the opening. We didn't see any deer, so we walked farther down the road to a point where we'd leave it and go in and get the buck.

Suddenly a bunch of deer flushed from cover and headed for the forest. For some reason, three deer stopped in the clearcut at the edge of the timber and stared at us. One of the deer was a small buck, but for the life of me I couldn't tell if it was a spike or forkhorn. The buck was about 250 yards away, and if he was a forkhorn at all, he was a small one.

The buck wouldn't turn his head so we could see what he was wearing. He stood as still as a statue, looking directly at us, which is why we couldn't make out the antler configuration.

I suggested to my pal that he try a sneak while we kept the buck's attention. I read many times in Jack O'Connor's sheep hunting stories that sheep can't count. When a bunch of them are staring at a group of hunters, one of the hunters can slip away and make a stalk. I was sure blacktails couldn't count either, and I had the feeling that the little buck wasn't going anywhere for a while.

In order to make the stalk, my companion had to drop down into a draw where he'd be out of sight of the buck. As the hunter made progress, he'd look back at me, and I'd direct him with hand signals.

It took him about 15 minutes to complete the stalk to the point where he could see the buck. My friend eased up to the top of the rise and peeked over the top. The buck was still there; no more than 40 yards away. I knew the hunter would spot the buck quickly, and was positive that the animal would be his, if it was a forkhorn. A shot might be imminent.

But no shot came, and the hunter wasn't looking toward the buck. I couldn't figure out what was going on. The hunter and buck were unbelievably close to each other, but nothing was happening. With my binoculars I saw my pal looking at me making a gesture that indicated he was needing advice. I answered by carefully and slowly moving my arm toward the direction of the deer. I didn't want to move too rapidly for fear of scaring the buck. The hunter turned his attention back to the deer, and I again anticipated a shot. Still it didn't come.

When the hunter gestured to me again, this time I gestured back by vigorously waving my hat toward the deer. This response was also unsuccessful. The deer was still standing as big as life, but my friend couldn't see him.

My next response to my pal's gesture was to direct him via a low, monotone shout.

"THE BUCK IS STILL IN THE SAME SPOT AS BEFORE", I said. I fully expected the deer to move when it heard my voice, but it stayed rooted to the spot.

Still the hunter couldn't see it, and when he gestured again, I raised my voice several octaves. "THE BUCK IS STILL THERE. LOOK TOWARD WHERE I'M POINTING."

Nothing. No luck. By this time I was getting frustrated big time. Now I was screaming. "THE BUCK IS RIGHT IN FRONT OF YOU, YOU DUMMY." (I knew my pal well enough that insults were not taken seriously, but part of our routine dialogue.)

The deer continued to stand throughout the commotion. Now I desperately wanted that buck killed, assuming it was a forkhorn. The more I looked at it, the more I thought it was. It wouldn't be good for the herd if the dumb deer passed on its obviously inferior genes. But my friend was still not seeing it.

"YOU JERK, ARE YOU BLIND? THE STUPID DEER IS STILL THERE," I shouted at the top of my voice.

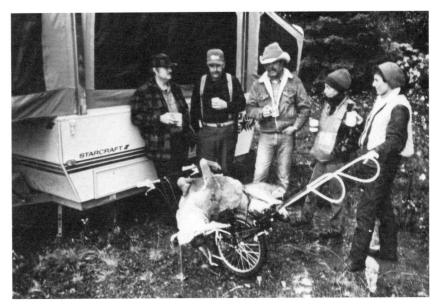

Our gang at deer camp. My companions make the hunt special. We don't need to kill big bucks to have a good time, or ANY bucks, for that matter.

For the first time my pal broke the silence and shouted back. He too was frustrated. "I CAN'T SEE IT," he yelled. "WHAT SHOULD I DO?" As soon as the hunter shouted, the staring contest between me and the buck was broken. It turned its head to look at the hunter, and for the first time I had a profile view of its antlers. It was indeed a forkhorn.

"IT'S A LEGAL BUCK," I screamed. "DO SOMETHING. GET UP ON TOP OF A STUMP. TAKE A COUPLE STEPS FORWARD. DO ANYTHING."

My buddy took a few steps, and that did it. The buck made two swift bounds and was swallowed up by the thick forest. Evidently a small pocket of brush hid the deer, or my friend was too inexperienced to see it. The animal blended perfectly with the surroundings, even though it was in the open.

Despite that little buck's actions, I'm convinced that the West Coast deer are exceedingly wary and far underrated. In Washington and Oregon, they're less favored than the Rocky Mountain muley which inhabits the more arid regions east of the Cascade Mountains. Hunters prefer the muley because he lives in more open country and owns bigger antlers.

Blacktails are a mule deer subspecies. The Columbian blacktail inhabits western forests from California through much of British Columbia, while the Sitka blacktail inhabits northern B.C. and Alaska. While their antlers are smaller than those of the Rocky Mountain muley, mature blacktail bucks often weigh more than 175 pounds live weight.

Hunting techniques are almost always associated with clearcuts, and for good reason. Coastal forests are incredibly thick, and the Cascades aren't much of an improvement. With few exceptions, blacktail country is mean and nasty.

I'm not done hunting blacktails. One of these years I intend to confront a big old boy in his gloomy environment, where soggy moss hangs from huge trees and the forest floor is two to five feet beneath twisted underbrush and slippery logs that lay like Pick-up sticks. In much of that country, you can't see your companion wearing hunter orange five yards away. That's what I call a nightmare tangle.

When it comes to deer, blacktails just might be the ultimate challenge. The more I hunt them, the more I believe it. If you're a whitetail or trophy mule deer hunter and scoff at that statement, challenge a blacktail buck in his timbered bailiwick, one on one.

Once you do, I'll wager you won't scoff any more. And I'm going back to that clearcut where I was screaming my fool head off at my buddy. I've decided that the little buck was deaf and a little blind; maybe both. If he survived, he ought to be a big buck now, and maybe I can get a big deaf blacktail buck. For sure I'm not batting too well on healthy big blacktail bucks.

By the way, my buddy hasn't said to heck with deer hunting yet. He's still looking for his first buck, and we're having a tough time coming up with another dumb deer.

Packing my buck out of the most magnificent part of the Rockies.

A PERFECT HUNT IN WYOMING

The trail ran along the length of the ridge for miles, in some of Wyoming's most magnificent high country. Scree slopes fell away from the mountaintops, down to where vodka-clear streams flowed swiftly through canyon bottoms. Sagebrush and grassy openings mingled with stands of Douglas fir, Engelmann spruce and alpine fir, forming a mosaic of splendid big game country that abounded with elk, mule deer, and moose.

Our search for big-racked bucks took us to the very highest ridges, where rimrock ledges and boulder-strewn outcrops decorated the ancient glacial cirques. Those scoured-out basins held some of the biggest mule deer in the west, and for good reasons. Only the most dedicated hunters would penetrate that brutal land, and there were no guarantees that a big buck would be the reward.

As I sat on my horse, looking over the incredible vistas in every direction, the thought of killing a big muley was far from my mind. I was too absorbed with the wild country to think about anything else, and though I've lived in the Rockies for almost three decades, the celebrated mountains never become too mundane, never to be taken for granted.

Lynn Madsen brought me back to reality when he broke the silence and suggested we ride up the trail. I nudged my horse with my heels, and watched the brushy slopes for feeding deer as we rode.

I was hunting Wyoming's Greys River area in the Bridger-Teton National Forest. The region is known for big muleys, and it's one of the few places in the state where you can hunt with a firearm in September. In the other units, seasons start in October or November, depending on the unit.

September hunting is unique, offering a completely different dimension to pursuing muleys. The hunts are in high elevations, usually in remote areas that require some hiking and climbing. The weather is often balmy, though a storm can quickly move in and temporarily dump heavy snow. Bucks are usually as high as they can get, provided there's adequate feed, and they tend to hang out in bachelor groups. It's not uncommon to see three or more big bucks together. And finally, light hunting pressure is the rule, rather than the exception. You might not hear a shot for days.

These factors, in addition to the fact that you're hunting the loveliest landscape in the west, make September hunting a splendid experience. A quality experience is assured, whether you kill a buck or not.

Lynn Madsen runs hunts with his father-in-law, Everett Petersen. Everett, who is a charter member of the Wyoming Outfitter's Association, and one of the finest veteran outfitters in the west, owns Petersen's Hunting and Fishing Camps out of Afton, Wyoming.

I'd heard of Everett over the years, and finally met him at a Sportsman's Show. I listened to some of his yarns, including an episode when he guided Jack O'Connor, and took an immediate liking to Everett. A soft-spoken man with an easy smile, he had a pleasant personality that was typically western.

Lynn guides for Everett in the fall, along with Randy, another of Everett's son-in-laws. The trio hunt out of two camps, one that you can drive to in a vehicle, and another that requires an easy two-hour horseback ride. I hunted out of the latter, a comfortable, clean camp nestled in a stand of evergreen trees under a lofty ridgetop.

This wasn't my first hunt in the Greys River area. In 1979, I made a solo trip, backpacking high in the mountains. That was a disappointing adventure, because energy exploration was at a frenzy in the west. Seismic crews seemed to be everywhere in the mountains, blasting lines to test for oil. Helicopters flew across the mountains and valleys from dawn to dusk, and I'd had enough after two days. I packed my mountain tent and gear and left for my home in Utah, promising to return when the countryside settled down.

Sometime later, my friend Gabby Barrus of Cody, Wyoming invited me to hunt the Greys River with him. Having drawn a nonresident permit in the lottery for the region, I accepted the invitation. We hunted with outfitter Grant Barrus (no relation to Gabby), during a mid-October hunt.

Gabby and I saw some big bucks, including two giants that eluded us in the fog, but we didn't score. Again I promised to return, and 10 years had passed when I met Everett and agreed to hunt out of his camp.

Though I'd been a resident of Cody, Wyoming, for five years, and normally hunt on my own in the state, there was no hesitation when the opportunity arose to hunt Greys River again. I've hunted all over the Rockies, but there was a special appeal in that part of western Wyoming.

Lynn and I rode about 15 miles that first day, glassing basins and brushy slopes. As we approached a likely place, we tied the horses well away from the area and eased up on foot. Through binoculars and spotting scopes, we looked at a number of bucks, but none were big enough to arouse our interest.

I wasn't determined to take a trophy-class buck, but wanted something respectable. Besides, I had five days to hunt, and didn't want to end it too quickly.

My chance at a big buck came late the second day. Lynn and I hiked into a remote canyon that had no access, and looked up the mountain to see five bucks staring down at us about 150 yards away. One was decidedly bigger than the others, but from the steep angle of view, I couldn't see his tines, just the main beams that appeared very wide.

My hesitation to evaluate him more thoroughly cost me the buck. While I looked at him with my binoculars, the herd suddenly bounded off and disappeared in the rimrock. In the second or two before they went out of sight, I saw a profile of his rack. He was a dandy, with four long, deep tines on each side. The other bucks had good racks, but not as good as the bigger animal.

Expecting the deer to show in the huge boulders, I took a dead rest on a log, but the bucks never appeared. They ran up a rocky chute, and quickly vanished over the ridgetop. There was no chance to scramble up for a look. Night was coming on, and by the time we got to the top the deer would be long gone.

The next day, Lynn and I saw more bucks, but nothing as big as the one that eluded us. Part of our strategy was to flush deer bedded in stunted spruce trees that grew at timberline. Bucks often used the trees for shelter during the daylight hours, but the spruces were thick enough that you had to practically walk up to a deer to get it up.

Lynn also tried driving deer out of timbered pockets, but big bucks weren't cooperative. In one huge, rocky basin, he made a three hour circle, walking through tiny patches of wind-bent spruces that were just six to eight feet high. I was posted on the opposite slope to intercept fleeing deer, and saw a number of deer go by that weren't particularly noteworthy.

Everett joined us the next day, and suggested we try making big drives through timbered areas with the other three hunters in camp. The other hunters and I would post ourselves in spots with good vantage points, while Everett, Lynn and Randy made the drives on horseback.

The first effort produced three bucks, several does and fawns, and some elk. Lynn saw a big buck, but the animal ran out through the flank and never showed himself to the standers. A bunch of elk crashed through the timber and ran straight toward me. I waited until they were about 10 yards away, and jumped up and waved my arms. I watched in amusement as a spike bull and a dozen cows and calves skidded to a halt and looked at me in wide-eyed surprise. They wasted no time gathering their wits and smashing their way back into the forest.

On the next drive, I was positioned just under a rimrock ledge where I had a commanding view of the slopes below. Any deer that spooked would almost have to run below me; the farthest shot would be about 250 yards.

The drive was 10 minutes old when I saw a buck running in my direction low on the slope. He was followed by two more, one of which seemed to be decent.

I had plenty of time to look over the bucks intently, even though they were bounding smartly along. All were four-pointers, but one had a bit more mass and a higher rack than the others. I knew he wasn't as big as the first buck I'd seen, but I made a quick decision to take him.

With the scope of my rifle centered on the bigger buck's chest, I saw the herd stop just under a ledge and look about in confusion. It appeared they'd winded another hunter who was on stand upwind.

I took advantage of the opportunity and fired, dropping the buck in

Me and my little buck (according to Everett). I should have shot the bigger one I saw earlier in the hunt. That's the way it goes.

his tracks. I judged him to be about 200 yards out.

The buck had four points to the side, and a spread of about 24 inches. His rack was high, which is what made him stand out from the others. As he ran, all I saw was a side view, unable to see the width of his antlers.

Everett was the first one to appear from the timber, and he had a grin on his face when he saw me standing next to the buck. When he approached the deer, his grin grew even wider.

"I thought you wanted a BIG buck," he said. "You should have held out for that little guy's grandpa."

"Every buck is a good buck," I joked. "Besides, I didn't think you grew 'em any bigger in this neck of the woods."

We traded a few more comments, and Lynn showed up. He was a bit easier on me, but reminded me of the big buck I'd passed on the first day. I think Lynn and Everett figured I was just a mite unhappy with the buck, but I was just as pleased as I would have been if the deer was much bigger.

To me, a representative animal of any species is worthy. I've let plenty of animals go by over my years of hunting, but I've never been a trophy hunter. It would be wonderful to put an animal in the record book, but that's not important to me. Besides, of the muley bucks I've killed around the west over the last three decades, several of them are in the 28 to 30-inch class.

After photographing the buck, we dressed and packed him to camp on a horse. It had been a perfect hunt for me, with plenty of camaraderie, a fine camp, beautiful country, and lots of game. Even the weather cooperated, which is always a nice bonus in the high country. As long as there are places like that to hunt, I'll never say to heck with deer hunting.

RATTLING IS EASY IN TEXAS

    A short time ago I was hankering for a Texas whitetail hunt. My good friend Murry Burnham was about to get a phone call. Murry is my Texas pal who owns the Burnham Brothers Co., which manufactures animal calls and other outdoor products. He is also a superb hunter, a man whose skills are unsurpassed in the deer woods.

"Are you sitting down?" he said as he answered the phone.

"What did you do now?" I kidded.

"Sold the business — to a heck of a nice young man. Name is Gary

Roberson, and he's quite a hunter," Murry said.

When we'd thoroughly discussed the end of Murry's long association with Burnham Brothers, we arranged a hunt. Murry, Gary and I would hunt in the Texas hill country, a region I'd always wanted to chase whitetails around in.

To Texans, the hill country is really the Edwards Plateau, a huge area that sprawls for thousands of square miles. It's loaded with deer, but doesn't have the monster whitetails that roam in south Texas. Make

Gary Roberson does his stuff. He's an excellent rattler and knows how to pull in bucks.

no mistake, Texans very definitely hold the south area on the highest pedestal when it comes to world-class whitetails. No other place in the state comes even close.

The hill country has traditionally raised so-so bucks, few of them very big. However, Gary set up a hunt on a ranch that produces some very nice bucks that raise eyebrows in that neck of the woods.

To the uninformed, if you want to hunt deer in Texas, you do one of three things. You hunt the very limited national forest land, competing with unbelievable numbers of hunters; you draw a tag in a lottery to hunt one of the very few state wildlife areas (odds of drawing a tag are woefully poor); or you pay to hunt private ranch land. Since 98 percent of Texas is private land, the latter option is far and away the most popular.

The ranch we hunted is owned by Lee Pfluger and Jack McJunkin, and was hunted only by friends of the owners. When I hunted with Gary, he hadn't yet begun a guide service, but intended to start the following season.

As deer camps go, this place was far from what I'm used to. A beautiful lodge on the Llanos River provided lovely accommodations. Ranch hands were available to process our deer, including skinning, boning, butchering, wrapping, freezing, and boxing it for the trip home. It was pampering at its best, and I'll admit it was very nice. Compared to most of my hunts in the Rockies, where I live, it was Five Star Rating; a whole lot more comfortable than half-freezing to death in a snowy elk camp, which I'm more accustomed to.

According to Gary, this camp produced some very large bucks for the hill country, primarily because the owners managed the land for big deer. Each hunter was required to take a doe and a spike buck, in addition to a trophy buck. In order to encourage hunters to take a spike, a beautifully engraved rifle is presented annually to the hunter who takes the spike with the longest antlers. By so doing, the ranch has an excellent composition of big bucks and does, and isn't overrun with too many dwarf deer as are many Texas ranches.

As luck would have it, a severe rainstorm struck the day before I arrived. Nonetheless, Gary and I drove out from the lodge well before sunup, fording a shallow spot on the Llanos River. Murry would join us that evening.

Our first attempt at rattling was enormously eventful. Gary had barely begun when a good buck trotted close for a look. He was a beauty, with a high, nine-point rack. I opted to pass, though I could easily have taken him at 40 yards with my .270.

The buck finally melted into the brush, and a spike suddenly appeared. Wanting to be a good guy and follow ranch rules, I dropped the little buck where he stood. I field dressed him and dragged him into the shade where we'd pick him up later.

The rest of the morning was absolutely amazing. Gary rattled from seven different locations, and pulled in bucks from five. By lunch time, I'd looked at eight different bucks, most of them six to eight-pointers. I passed on all of them. It was the first day of the hunt, and I didn't want to end it so soon.

At one point that morning, the rain beat down so incredibly hard that we took shelter in a well-constructed blind that was mercifully close to where we happened to be when the downpour started.

We headed back to the lodge for lunch after picking up my spike, but soon discovered that we couldn't cross the river. It had risen three feet; a huge set of rapids replaced the shallow ford that we'd crossed early that morning.

As we looked at the swollen, flooded river, we saw Jack paddling a small boat from the far side. We were rescued, and learned that much of Texas was flooded. Murry was unable to reach the ranch because roads were closed by high water.

Undaunted by the flooded river, we used the boat to cross, and Gary continued to rattle in bucks. I took a doe, again following the wishes of the landowners, and finally lowered the boom on a fine buck the next day.

It happened when we set up next to a wire fence, about an hour before dark. A few minutes after Gary began rattling, we were startled by a heavy thump behind us. At the same time, we heard the loud twang of wire. Though Gary and I were 20 feet apart, we knew exactly what had happened. A deer had jumped the fence just a few yards away. The noise was caused by its feet striking the top wire.

I turned to see a fine buck circling us. Gary whispered that he was a good one, and I wasted no time. Moments later we approached my buck. He was most pleasing, with a heavy nine-point rack.

The next day, Gary rattled in a buck from at least 800 yards out. We saw him coming, and he didn't stop until he was 50 yards away. Gary made an excellent shot on the very good buck, also a nine pointer.

A couple other things happened on that hunt that I hesitate to mention, but I'll do it anyway. Every now and then a guy ought to be able to poke fun at himself.

After I got my deer, Gary suggested we try for turkeys. Only gobblers were legal, and the limit was two.

Before daybreak the next morning we eased toward a big roost area along the river bottom that held at least 100 birds. We hunkered down behind a tree and waited. This was to be an ambush. I was using my .270, and hoped to intercept the birds as they walked from the roost to the feeding areas. Using rifles for turkeys is common in Texas and much of the west. It's illegal in many eastern states, and some folks think it's downright sacrilegious as well.

Nonetheless, I was poised for action, and it came soon after the birds flew down and walked toward us. At least four dozen hens went by, the farthest only 75 yards out, but there wasn't a longbeard among them.

Presently I spotted five gobblers, real dandies with beards 8 to 9 inches long. As they approached, I drew a bead on one and was about to pull the trigger when another gobbler walked closely beside it. I got a bright idea and decided to take them both with one bullet if they'd line up just right. They did, or I THOUGHT they did, but they really didn't, because at the shot they immediately flew away, leaving only a couple feathers as evidence of their presence.

"I think you missed." Gary said. He said it politely, but I'd rather he had kicked me in the butt.

"I tried to get 'em both with one shot," I said. "How could I miss?"

Evidently the bullet had passed directly between them, barely cutting a couple feathers from each bird.

With the turkey hunt over, we decided to try for a mouflon ram. Several sheep lived in one of the pastures, and the owners wanted them eliminated. Gary claimed they were elusive, and the pasture was covered with thick brush. He said we'd be lucky to find one.

We drove into the pasture, intending to follow a fence line; then park the vehicle and still hunt through the brush. Suddenly a bunch of mouflon sheep appeared along the fence line ahead of us. Evidently they'd been bedded, and we caught them by surprise.

One was a good ram. I jumped out, took a solid rest on a tree, and centered the bead on the ram's chest. Then I had a brief but disturbing thought.

I pose with the buck that Gary rattled in. He wasn't a bad whitetail for Texas's Hill Country.

"What do we do with the meat if I kill this sheep?" I whispered to Gary as I was in the process of squeezing the trigger.

"Don't know," he said. "Maybe one of the hands back at the ranch will take it."

I thought about the three deer in the freezer. I had plenty of venison, and really didn't need to take this critter. I also didn't know if the sheep was much good to eat. Neither did Gary. Maybe another time I'd take a mouflon sheep. I wasn't ready to claim it.

On the way back to the lodge, I whined a great deal about missing turkeys and not shooting the ram. At one point, Gary stopped to check a feeder. Something enormous was directly under it. In a flash, Gary grabbed his rifle, and seconds later a huge wild boar hit the ground. It was the biggest boar I'd seen, with enormous tusks. As a native Texan, Gary had taken plenty of boars, but this was his biggest. The owners of the ranch wanted them eradicated, and in fact had traps set out for them.

I'm going back to hunt that ranch with Gary. When I do, I'll try for one turkey at a time, and I'm never going to say to heck with mouflon rams again. I have some brand new chili recipes that I want to try.

Dan's first buck. I was a mighty proud Dad that day.

BLUE MOUNTAIN DID IT AGAIN

SIR... DANNY!

Hunting is an activity that produces plenty of memories. Some fade away with time, and some remain as vivid as the moments the hunt occurred. Perhaps the most memorable of all our hunts are those that involved our children's first hunting trip.

Elsewhere in this book I describe the first deer my two oldest daughters had taken. They evoke nostalgic thoughts now, just as they did then. The same is true with my son, Dan. His first hunt was a special experience, just as his sister's were. I'll never forget any of those wonderful hours in the woods with my children.

Dan's first deer hunt was in Colorado. We were Utah residents at the time, but Colorado allowed youngsters to hunt big game at an earlier age. I made a deal with Dan; he'd have to come up with half the nonresident fee, and I'd come up with the other half. As I recall, the tag was around $100. Dan had a part-time job after school sweeping floors in an auto dealership garage. He loved to be around mechanics when he was a youngster. It paid off; now he's an engineer for McDonnell Douglas, the aircraft manufacturer.

Dan was no stranger to firearms and hunting prior to his first deer hunt. Starting when he was just a toddler, he accompanied me on all sorts of hunts, from small game to waterfowl to big game. When he reached legal hunting age, he hunted cottontails, and easily collected a limit of head-shot bunnies taken with his scope-sighted .22.

By the time he was old enough to hunt deer, he knew how to accurately shoot his .243, and was wise to the ways of muleys as well. He'd accompanied me on more than a dozen deer hunts through the years.

Our hunting area was Blue Mountain that I've thoroughly described in another chapter. This mountain looms up out of the valley floor on the Utah-Colorado border, and supports an excellent population of muleys. Blue Mountain was a special place for me; I killed my first deer on it in the early 60's. That's why it was only fitting that Danny should also take his first buck on Blue Mountain.

We had our hunting area selected long before the hunt. One of Blue's slopes is choked with thick brush. It always harbored deer, and a hike from the roads kept a lot of hunters away.

It was still pitch black when we arrived. With the impending sunrise came a bit of snow, which was just right for hunting.

We sat on a rock jutting out from the mountain where we wouldn't be skylined. Almost immediately we started seeing deer in the improving light. They were everywhere; at least two dozen were in sight, most of them feeding here and there, others walking toward their daytime bedding areas.

Suddenly a small buck appeared. He walked up the mountain toward our location, and when he was about 125 yards away, Dan was ready. Steadied on a rock, he touched the trigger of his .243, just as he'd done dozens of times with his .22. And, just as before, his bullet was right on target. This time the quarry wasn't a cottontail; it was a muley buck. Dan had shot it squarely through the heart.

It was a small buck, but to a boy on his first deer hunt, it was the biggest trophy buck in all of Colorado. There was a lot of whooping and hollering on the mountain as we ran crazily to the fallen deer, and we went through the ritual that all my kids are familiar with. I smeared a dab of the buck's blood on Dan's face. He was now blooded, a proven hunter. In my eyes, the rite was just as significant as a knight being initiated into knighthood.

Dan insisted on dressing the buck himself. I didn't argue, and let him perform the chore. Besides, something was in my eye, I guess, because there were tears rolling down my cheek. I walked away and wiped my eyes. Must have been irritated by the doggoned wind. That same doggoned wind came up every time one of my kids killed their first buck: when Janette got hers in Utah, Judi got hers in Wyoming, and Danny got his in Colorado.

Dragging the buck down the mountain was easy. Filled with adrenalin, we had him to the truck in no time.

I looked back at Blue Mountain fondly as we left the dirt road and turned onto the highway. Two bucks for two boys, about 17 years apart.

Two bucks that will never be forgotten.

I almost lost this buck after I shot him. The toilet tissue I left to mark his location in the brush blew away. I'll never do that again.

YOU DID WHAT IN THE RAIN GAUGE?

(Definitly NOT A ~~____~~ L.B.B.)

I'm convinced that the Book Cliffs region in eastern Utah and western Colorado was created for mule deer. The area is a plateau that stretches for hundreds of square miles on both sides of the Utah-Colorado border, and is well-known for the deer that inhabit it. One thing is for certain — the Book Cliffs is no well-kept secret. Thousands of hunters comb it annually in search of a muley.

I've hunted the Books, as it is called locally, more consistently then any other part of the west. I lived in Vernal, Utah for 11 years, and in Price, Utah for two years. Vernal is a few dozen miles north of the Books; Price is a few dozen miles to the southwest.

It was the Book Cliffs that provided me the opportunity of moving west after working at West Point for 8 years. A job as a wildlife biologist opened up with the Bureau of Land Management in Vernal, and I received the offer after I applied. The job itself was technically titled

"Oil Shale Wildlife Biologist", which, I soon found out, meant studying the fish and game that inhabited an area underlain with rich deposits of oil shale. In those days, the federal government and several of our biggest oil companies were trying to figure ways of extracting the oil from the shale with a minimum of disturbance, but mostly to do it cost effectively. The BLM, a Department of Interior agency, managed most of the land that had oil shale beneath it, and came through with some funding to research wildlife on those lands.

I studied all critters on the oil rich areas, from birds to cottontails to muleys and elk. When I first started, some of the birds were identified as LBB's (little brown birds — because I wasn't sure as to their species).

Funding for the job ran out a year later and I became a Book Cliffs wildlife biologist, which meant that I was involved in wildlife throughout the entire Books rather than just the oil shale area.

It was easy to fall in love with the Book Cliffs, especially when you worked there year-round, seeing its many moods and secrets that you didn't see when the area was mobbed by hunters, which happened every year.

The region isn't particularly beautiful as the high country goes. There are no snow-capped peaks, no clear, rushing streams, no mountain lakes and timbered basins. It is simply a high plateau choked with some of the best deer habitat I've ever seen. Thick patches of oak brush grow extensively throughout, with clumps of mountain mahogany, serviceberry, bitterbrush, and other plants that shelter and feed deer. Broad sagebrush areas blanket the landscape, interspersed with tight pinon-juniper forests at lower elevations. In the higher reaches, Douglas fir, ponderosa pine and spruce grow in intermittent stands, surrounded by lovely glades of quaking aspen. If ever a place screamed muleys, it was the Books.

Over the years, I took many deer from the region, including some of my best bucks. My first bow-killed deer came from the Books, when I was working as a forester out of Price in the mid-60's.

I'll never forget one particularly incredible scene on that hunt. Before my eyes I saw more than 20 very big muley bucks running single file through the aspens. It was an awesome spectacle as buck after buck, all of them wearing at least four points to the side, bounded across the aspen forest. How I wished that it was firearms season and that I had a rifle in my hands instead of the bow when the deer herd waltzed by at

60 yards.

Sometime later I saw a big doe slipping through the aspens about 20 yards away. Since there was a bag limit of two deer and I needed the meat, I waited for the doe to walk behind a tree, drew my bowstring, and loosed an arrow.

The shot looked good, but it happened so fast I wasn't sure of a hit. I searched the ground for 10 minutes and finally located a spot of blood as big as a B-B. I walked in the direction of the doe's flight and found her lying dead in a small depression. She'd gone 60 yards.

When I worked for the BLM in Vernal, I frequently stayed at one of the government cabins in the Books while doing big game studies. The BLM had cabins, and so did the Utah Division of Wildlife Resources, the state wildlife agency. Most of our work involved winter range surveys, and I have vivid memories of some interesting evenings between dinner and bedtime. The older wardens would share tales, many of which were hard to believe, but undoubtedly true.

One interesting tale that I'll never forget related an incident when a warden watched four deer hunters walking across a sagebrush flat toward a clump of aspens. The warden whistled to the hunters to get their attention, and waved them over. The men continued walking to the aspens where they momentarily disappeared. Presently they emerged from the other side and walked over to the warden. One of the men wasn't carrying a rifle, but he had one slung over his shoulder when he entered the trees. Wardens don't miss seeing those details when they're observing people.

When they approached, the warden asked to check their licenses. Three of them came up with their licenses, but the fourth man balked.

"I wasn't huntin'," the man said. "I was just walkin' with my buddies."

"That's funny," the warden responded. "I swore I saw all four of you carrying rifles."

"Wasn't huntin'," the man insisted.

The warden was a veteran in the business, and he wasn't believing the story. He had the little mystery easily figured out: when the men spotted the warden, one of them had no license. Rather than face a fine, he stashed his rifle in the aspens, intending to return for it later.

Since the man seemed to be adamant about his innocence, the warden told them to make themselves comfortable while he took a little walk to the aspens.

Book Cliffs bucks are wary because of the hunting pressure. You need to get back away from roads and hunt in thick cover when there's lots of competition from other hunters.

It didn't take long for the lawman to find what he was looking for. There, propped against a tree, was a beautiful .270 rifle. It was an expensive custom-made job, with one of the best scopes on the market.

He carried the firearm back to the four hunters.

"Mighty nice rifle I found, boys," he said. "Must have cost a lot of money. Somebody must have plumb forgot it in those trees. Anybody here recognize it?"

The men shrugged and mumbled, kicking at clods in the dirt.

The warden walked up to the man who claimed he wasn't hunting, and held the rifle up.

"You sure this ain't your rifle, son? Maybe you forgot it in the aspens?"

"Ain't mine," the man responded. "I wasn't huntin', and I ain't never seen that gun before."

"Have it your way," the warden said, "but I'll make you a deal. I'm going to take this rifle home. If you decide that maybe it's yours after all, call me. You'll get your gun back, but it will cost you a ticket for hunting without a license."

"It ain't my damned gun," the man said nervously. "Do whatever you want with it."

"Okay," the warden answered. "I'll keep it in my house for one year. If you haven't called me by then, I'll turn it in to my office and we'll auction it with the rest of our confiscated evidence."

The warden gave the man his address and phone number, but never received a call. He checked with other law enforcement agencies; the gun wasn't stolen. The rifle was auctioned in the state sale, and that was that.

As I worked in the Book Cliffs, I saw plenty of big bucks, but the area was being quickly developed by oil and gas companies in their frantic search for rich deposits. This was about the time of the energy crunch, when gasoline prices skyrocketed and we all had to wait our turn for fuel in long lines at the gas station.

To meet the energy crunch, companies worked at a feverish pace, drilling everywhere they could — in canyon bottoms and on ridgetops. Of course, every place they drilled they built a big, sprawling road to the site.

When the drilling was done, there were roads on practically every ridge and down every major canyon. The Books were opened up in a big way, and deer hunters had access to an enormous part of the region.

Some of my favorite spots, places heavily vegetated with thick pockets of brush, were bulldozed away. Those brushy areas offered prime shelter to big bucks, but those havens were gone. In one spot that was entirely eliminated from the planet, I'd killed three big four-point bucks. I could always count on it to produce a good deer, but when the bulldozers got done it was only a memory.

On one particular hunt, I was with three pals who were only

mediocre hunters. Hunting was more or less a casual pastime; it didn't matter to them whether they got a deer or not. That was fine with me; everyone does their own thing, but I wasn't about to partake in the late-night poker game they'd involved themselves in the night before the season. As they played and I tried to sleep as far from the table as possible, one of them admitted that his wife was not too happy with his weekend deer hunt. To placate her poor attitude, he'd sent her a dozen roses and promised he'd hunt only on opening day.

What a guy. I never could figure why he came out to hunting camp in the first place. Maybe he needed a night playing cards with the boys.

When the card game droned on long into the night, I went out and slept in the cab of my pickup truck. I've been known to partake of numerous late night card games in deer camp myself, but those were in my younger days. I guess I outgrew that form of socializing, but only when I'm in hunting camp. I'm a sucker for a poker game almost any other time. On that hunt, as on all my hunting trips, I intended to be in the woods long before shooting light. I'd located some good bucks before the season, and wanted to be there at the crack of dawn.

It was an hour before sunrise when I headed out from camp afoot. I got to the area where I knew bucks would probably be feeding, and hunkered down next to a juniper tree to wait for shooting light.

Ten minutes later I heard a truck coming. I wasn't surprised, because I expected all kinds of hunters in the area. This truck, however, stopped smack in the middle of the place that I'd been watching. The driver pulled off the road and drove through the sage for 300 yards, as if he intentionally planned to screw things up. He didn't bother to get out of the truck, and I figured correctly that he'd sit in the warm cab and wait for sunlight.

I heard other vehicles as well, and in the dark I could see headlights and taillights weaving about on other adjoining ridges. It was a typical Utah opening day in the Books. I estimated that probably 75 percent of the hunters road-hunted at some time during opening weekend, and that 25 percent road-hunted exclusively. By road hunting, I mean slowly driving about, looking for game. If a legal animal is spotted, the hunter simply jumps out and fires, hopefully following the laws in regard to the direction he's shooting and the distance he is from the vehicle or roadway.

With my primary strategy ruined by the people in the truck, I hurriedly went to Plan Number 2, which was to get up on a rock overlooking a brushy basin, where spooked deer would be running through in order to reach escape cover.

With the arrival of daylight came several deer sneaking through the brush. Two small bucks accompanied a half-dozen does and fawns, but I let the bucks go.

Hunters were now everywhere. Gunshots rang out from every direction, and you could see humans clad in total hunter orange from

This buck was one of several I got from the same general area. It's an advantage to be familiar with the area you're hunting.

waist up almost anyplace you looked. A new hunting season was born, and with it the usual pandemonium and carnival-like atmosphere.

I was walking along the rim of a ridge when I saw a pair of hunters tossing rocks into a steep, brushy sidehill. They were about 100 yards away, so I stopped and watched. They moved on and disappeared, and suddenly I heard something busting brush below the rim toward my position.

Moments later two bucks boiled over the rim, bounding smartly across an old burned area that was conveniently devoid of trees. I drew down on what looked to be the biggest buck and dropped him nicely in his tracks. He wasn't huge, but had a tight rack with five points to the side.

I dressed the buck, and walked back to camp with a fresh liver. Upon arriving I noted that my card-playing companions were still snoozing. It was 8 a.m., and when I awoke them with the smells of liver, onions, eggs and pancakes, they initially didn't believe I'd killed a buck so soon.

Not surprisingly, they went home without a deer, but they had a good time anyway. Different strokes for different folks, as they say. Hunting is what you want it to be.

Another time I killed a good four-point buck in the Books, but I wasn't happy with the requirement of transporting him out of the nasty basin he fell in. My son Danny was with me, so I had him help me plan a route. He was about 12, not much help in dragging, but enough so it wasn't a total ordeal to move the buck. Every now and then I'd have him scout ahead to find the best path in which to drag the buck.

At one point he was about 50 yards ahead in the brush, yelling to me about the best route to take. I shouted back, and decided to walk up and take a look. The truck was parked on an old road, and I wanted to precisely pinpoint the road location since I didn't want to drag the buck one more inch uphill than I had to.

As I approached Danny, after shouting back and forth a few more times over his location, we were both shocked when a big buck exploded from cover not three yards from where Danny was standing.

I was amazed. That buck had lain quietly in heavy brush while Danny had been screaming at me. It was a good lesson, one that I've never forgotten. Since then, I've had other big muley bucks do the same thing, and I'm convinced they're expert at hiding. That knowledge helped me to be more thorough in my hunting efforts.

I was still recovering from the buck's startling flush when four big guys walked over and asked if I needed help dragging the buck. They were from Arkansas, and a congenial bunch of men. Before I could politely refuse, they grabbed hold of the buck and quickly had him to the road. They refused a hindquarter for their efforts, but they joined me in some dessert around the campfire that night. I've made some fine acquaintances in hunting camps. Those men were good company, like most hunters I've known.

Another time I was hunting the Books with a non-hunting companion who sat in the car at one point because of a bad blister. I hiked toward a thicket of oak brush, and when I topped a ridge I spotted a very good buck with his head down, feeding in the vegetation. I dropped him at 40 yards, and had him field dressed within 20 minutes.

He was too big to drag out alone, so I headed back to the car to get my accomplice. Before leaving, I marked the buck's location with a square of toilet tissue that I pierced on a limb about seven feet off the ground. The scrub oak was so thick that I figured I'd have trouble finding the buck unless I marked the spot where he lay.

Upon returning with my friend, I couldn't find the toilet tissue. We looked everywhere, first for the tissue, and then for the buck. I realized that the tissue must have been blown off by the wind.

A half hour of searching still didn't produce the buck, and I was mad at myself. How does one lose a big muley buck on the side of a mountain? It was unbelievable.

Suddenly I saw a pair of magpies fly into a clump of heavy brush. That was it. Magpies are known to be great detectives to game wardens because they betray the presence of a gut pile or a carcass that would otherwise go unseen.

I headed straight for the birds, and there was my deer. I was relieved, but my joy soon gave way to great pain and suffering as we inched the big buck back to the car. It was an ordeal, but when I was in my sleeping bag that night, I decided it was worth it.

Another Book Cliffs hunt that I'll never forget occurred the last couple days of the routine 11-day Utah hunting season. I'd left my camp trailer in the mountains after the opener, intending on hunting out of it the last of the season. I didn't do any good the first few days; having passed on a few mediocre bucks.

I like to hunt quaking aspens whenever I can. This picture shows why.

When I returned to the camper with two pals, the roads were a mess, covered with 15 inches of fresh snow. I had to chain up all four tires on my 4WD pickup to get to the camp. What a difference! A few days before it was dry and dusty; now it was a winter wonderland.

Early the next morning I was able to drive only a mile up the road. It was blocked by deep snow, but I was close to where I wanted to hunt anyway.

I trudged through knee deep snow, anticipating a great day. In my opinion, snow is a deer hunter's delight, since you can follow tracks and see deer better. As a bonus, deep snow pushes deer out of the high elevations and into lower winter range. They're concentrated in a much smaller area and are more accessible.

I hadn't seen a single deer, not even a doe, an hour after shooting light. It seemed that the ridges that were full of deer the week before were now totally devoid of deer, as if they suddenly disappeared.

Soon I learned that they did just that. I came across deep trails in the snow made by dozens of deer. The trails, less than 12 hours old, seemed to lead off every ridge, down every canyon. Small trails ran into bigger trails, until they funneled into very large major trails. All the tracks, without exception, were heading down the mountain toward winter range areas.

I knew exactly what had happened. I'd just missed a major migration, and it was truly major. I'd yet to see one of that magnitude, and I couldn't help wondering what I would have seen if I had been there when the deer were moving out.

I followed the trails for two miles. It was tough going; I was able to maintain a reasonable pace only by walking in the packed-down trail made by the deer. If I stepped outside, my foot plummeted into two feet of snow. By midafternoon I gave up, realizing that the deer were too far to catch up to. I headed back to camp.

My buddies had witnessed the same scenario where they'd hunted. The mountain simply gave up its deer herd in a few hours time.

A quick consultation at dinner resulted in a change of plans. We'd pull camp early in the morning and try to ambush the deer on their way to winter range.

It was a good idea, but it didn't work. The muleys had beaten us down. We hunted the area for a day and decided to move lower yet — smack in the middle of winter range.

We hit the jackpot on the next move. Deer were everywhere. By 8 o'clock that morning I'd seen 125 deer. I collected a nice buck in a bunch of juniper trees, and my buddies each scored as well. To this day I'll never forget the sight of those countless trails funneling off that mountainside.

A rather hilarious story is told about a man who worked for the government and was responsible for managing the Book Cliffs area. He was a likable chap, and he was immensely proud of the Books that he knew so well. He was so proud, in fact, that he claimed the Books were a unique "Banana Belt" in that otherwise arid part of Utah. He said it was true because his rain gauges were always full, or nearly so, yet no one else could account for that phenomenon.

The story that I heard from somewhat reliable sources, was that a few old cowboys enjoyed playing practical jokes and relieved themselves in the rain gauges. This may or may not be true, but knowing the bizarre sense of humor of a few cowboys I'm acquainted with, I wouldn't doubt it. Maybe it gets pretty boring out on the range, and it's necessary to make fun where you can find it.

The Books continue to be one of Utah's most popular deer hunting areas today. Many hunters lament that the big bucks have been shot out, but I'm convinced there are quite a few big old boys who know how to survive. I frequently think of the buck that Danny almost stepped on, and others that I've seen do similar things.

Though I live a long way from the Books now, I haven't said to heck with them yet. I want to go back to try again. Maybe I won't see a big buck, but it'll be fun reliving years of great memories. Nostalgia is a wonderful part of hunting.

WHEN THE BADLANDS AREN'T BAD

A good chunk of western real estate is badlands. This name was probably adopted because the bad guys hid out in them when the sheriff's posse was hot on their tails. Or maybe the name came about because most folks didn't figure the badlands were good for much of anything.

The badlands are really lowland areas with lots of gullies, draws, sparse brush, and few trees. Some of them are a nasty maze of eroded hills and weird formations. Because of the topography and hiding places, plenty of deer live in them — both whitetails and muleys.

One year, I hunted a badland area in Wyoming not far from my home in Cody. I hiked from dawn until noon, and saw only a small forked-horn buck and a few does.

Because of the clay and sandy soil in the badlands, tracks were readily imprinted, but I couldn't locate the animals that made them.

I consulted a topo map and noted a small spring about two miles away. Assuming deer would be watering at it, I headed in that direction.

I was close to the spring when I routinely glassed a high, rocky outcrop across a wide draw. A brief flash of light caught my eye, and I trained my binoculars on it. Through the heat waves, a fine buck materialized. He was among some boulders, lying partially in the shade.

The only route was to make a wide circle, crossing the draw and coming up behind the buck. The wind was typically blowing upslope, so it wouldn't cause problems.

Before leaving, I pinpointed the buck's exact location by noting the configuration of rocks on the skyline. I knew that when I came in from the opposite direction, I'd need to have a conspicuous landmark to guide me to the deer.

It took me almost two hours to make the circle. As I approached the spot, I eased ahead cautiously, taking care to avoid making the slightest sound in the rocks.

Carefully I peered over the last ledge with my rifle ready. No buck. I moved forward, slowly inching my way along, until I was sure I was looking at the spot where he'd been bedded.

Figuring the deer had possibly spotted me as I crossed the open draw, I slipped forward a few more feet. Suddenly I heard a noise around the bend, and saw the buck as it lunged to its feet and dashed out of sight.

I scrambled over the top, but the deer was gone, eluding me by running through the maze of rocks below. I'd seen enough to know he was huge, one of the biggest bucks I'd ever seen in 25 years of hunting them.

When I was done cussing myself, I looked the area over closely, and was amazed to find that the buck had bedded in at least three locations, each of them a dozen or so yards apart. I guessed that he'd rebedded to avoid the sun's direct rays, seeking shade as the sun moved.

Hunting badlands is a unique opportunity, being essentially a glassing and stalking exercise. Though deer usually aren't as numerous in badland areas as in more traditional spots, they often grow old and large because of the limited hunting pressure.

One of the most proven strategies is to get into the hunting area before first light, looking for deer from a high vantage point as soon as it's light enough to see. It's often possible to watch deer bed down, and then make a careful stalk.

Bucks prefer to bed in ledges and rocks, usually just under a rim where they can see below. Good visibility seems to be an important consideration when a buck selects its bed.

Because badland regions seldom support vast areas of adequate forage, deer concentrate their feeding efforts in places that yield sufficient browse, such as sagebrush, bitterbrush, and saltbush. Water is also critical, but muleys will commonly walk several miles for a drink.

Most western states have badlands, which are unique geological areas of thin, shallow soils, upthrusted rocky outcrops, and arid climates. Much of the land in these regions is administered by the U.S. Bureau of Land Management, a federal agency that allows free public hunting.

Both Dakotas have large areas as badlands, and there are extensive areas in Montana, Wyoming, Idaho, Colorado, Nevada, and Utah. Some areas support juniper forests, and some are covered with mountain mahogany and pinon pine.

Some advantages of hunting badlands include the lack of other hunters, plenty of public land, and good visibility. My primary motivations are the huge bucks that sneak around the rocks and dry gulches, and I like the idea of hunting in a place shunned by other hunters.

I remember a Wyoming deer hunt with outdoor humorist Pat

Jack Atcheson Sr. and I with my badlands buck. We saw dozens of bucks in eastern Montana during that hunt.

Jack Atcheson Sr. and I got in a short sage grouse hunt after finishing our deer hunt. I say "short" because there were jillions of grouse. It was a quick and easy bird hunt.

McManus. We chose to hunt a small badland region adjacent to a national forest that was hammered by plenty of hunters who drove by the desolate badlands without giving it the slightest consideration. We found a surprising number of deer in the barren landscape, and had the whole area to ourselves, even though it was public land.

One year I hunted Montana's badland country with Jack Atcheson Sr., my good hunting buddy who is also one of the top hunting consultants and booking agents in the world. He is as avid a hunter as I've ever met, and loves to chase muleys in the vast eastern part of his home state.

It was just the right time to hunt muleys. The rut was in full swing and groups of deer were everywhere. Our hunting mode was to drive the unbelievably barren countryside where you never saw another human all day, and glass for deer. We had no trouble finding them, and I finally dropped a modest 3 by 4 muley the last day of the hunt.

Practically every herd of does and fawns had a buck tending them; if they didn't a buck showed up sooner or later, almost at a trot. That was a great hunt — lots of deer and plenty of Big Sky country to hunt in.

And somewhere out there, in northwest Wyoming, a huge buck may still be sneaking around in his quiet, undisturbed hideaway. I hope so, because I intend to tie my tag to his enormous rack.

I have a score to settle in the badlands, which really aren't bad at all.

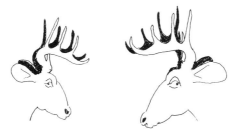

Judi and her first buck. You can tell she was a happy lady that day in Wyoming.

A BIG DAY FOR JUDI

The dirt road weaves through the eroded, arid hills of Wyoming's badlands, and I drive slowly, carefully avoiding sharp rocks that are betrayed by my pickup's headlights.

The panel lights inside the cab illuminate Judi's face just enough to reveal her attentiveness. It's opening day of deer season, and she'll hunt her first buck today.

"It's getting light, Dad," she says. "Will we be late?"

I look over to the east and see the brightening skies, but we're on schedule. By first light I figure we'll be at a good vantage point to look for deer in the seemingly barren wastelands.

Smiling to myself, I reassure my daughter that we'll be on time. I know that there aren't many 16-year old kids around who appreciate the need to be hunting at first shooting light. Few teenagers have ever looked to the east in the predawn hours, anticipating the excitement of the outdoor morning to come.

Judi has been on enough hunts with me that she understands the critical points. Now it's her turn to worry about such matters.

Presently we arrive at the top of a ridge that separates the hunting units. Judi's unit is mostly federal land, a vast desert area that is beat out by too much domestic sheep grazing.

Typical of many western public lands, the landscape barely supports vegetation — what is there grows sparsely, somehow wringing enough moisture from the eroded soil to hold on. Sagebrush and other plants grow in low clumps. There is not a tree or a high bush for 30 miles in any direction.

The low vegetation presents a tough hunting challenge. No screening cover will hide us. We'll have to use the intricacies of the topography to stalk the quarry. Hunting the badlands seems simple because of the openness of the country. In reality, it is seldom easy. Stalking must be done with precision, and loose rocks and varying winds offer complications.

I make the mistake of driving over the ridge. My plan is to park my pickup and start hiking, but almost immediately I spot a half dozen tell-tale rumps on a distant knoll.

The light is too poor to see much, and the animals are too far to see antlers with binoculars. I know the deer can see the truck, but I hope they're so far away they don't care. Muleys usually have a safety range of about 600 yards. Any closer and they get nervous.

Rather then move the truck out of sight, I leave it where it is. Otherwise the muleys will be unsettled. Open-country animals such as deer and antelope are often secure if they can see danger at a long distance.

Judi looks at the deer with binoculars as I set up the spotting scope. She comments that the animals are probably all does, though she concedes that the muleys are so far that antlers might not be visible.

"There's your buck," I say to my daughter, "if you want him. He's a nice little three-point — no monster, but a pretty good deer."

Judi looks through the scope and makes a quick decision. "I want him, Dad. He's plenty big for me."

I size up the country and plan a stalk. This is rolling land, with lots of knolls separated by gulches. We'll have to make a big circle by traveling in the bottoms.

The stalk will be a challenge. Once we get down in the gullies, everything will look different. As we move, I'll have to make several guesses as to our location, always figuring where the deer are. From our vantage point, I can't see beyond a low ridge between the deer and us. I don't know what's out there; we'll find out when we start walking.

The only landmark is an old fence line about 200 yards from the deer. The wires are gone; it consists only of a few rotted cedar posts stuck in the dry soil. I'm not sure I can see the posts from the gully, but I plan a mental route that will hopefully take us to them unobserved by the deer.

I check the wind, and we set out. We turn around and walk away from the deer, making it obvious to them that we're leaving.

As we descend out of sight, I take one more look through binoculars. The animals all appear to be feeding, unalarmed at our presence.

Judi carefully chambers a round in the .243 Remington. I watch as she slips on the safety and eases her way down the sloping hill.

"You nervous, kid?" I whisper.

"Yes," she answers. "I'll probably miss."

"That's the wrong attitude," I say. "You need to think positive. You're going home with your first buck today."

She smiles and reaches for my hand. We hold hands for a while, and I don't dare tell her I'm nervous, too. There are a lot of "what ifs" to think about. My worst fear is that she'll wound the buck. I strike the thought from my mind and we continue on.

As I expected, the country looks drastically different from the bottom of the drainages. I try to visualize where we are in relation to the deer, looking for the old fence line at every opportunity, but I can't see it.

Finally I decide it's time to sneak a peek. Judi and I carefully work our way up a knoll, taking care not to loosen rocks with our boots. It's tough to move quietly in the dry, rocky terrain.

We inch our way up, and I see the deer, but they're still too far out. They're feeding, but I see only three. The buck isn't there.

I assume the deer are bedding for the day, and I spot the old fence line. We still have a long way to go. The distance is short as the crow flies, but our meandering route along the gullies requires us to make a lengthy stalk.

Once again we walk along the bottoms, and this time I'm more positive of our location. Judging from my new perspective of the landform, we might be able to get within 100 yards of the deer, maybe closer.

We walk another 10 minutes, picking our way slowly. In some places the gullies are deeply washed out, forcing us to walk on the steep sidehills.

It's now time to make the final approach. Before we head up, I whisper last minute suggestions. I tell Judi to take a position where she can rest the rifle while shooting, and remind her to relax and draw a fine bead as she squeezes the trigger.

Her expression is serious and intense. She manages to flash a smile, but it's short-lived.

Judi has tagged along with me on many big game hunts over the years. When she was 11, she shot bedded jackrabbits with a scope-sighted .22. At 12, when she passed her hunter's safety course and got her small game license, she neatly drilled sitting cottontails with amazing consistency.

I hoped her past experiences would pay off. A buck mule deer is vastly different from a rabbit or hare. Antlers have a unique way of befuddling the brain, no matter how well prepared for the confrontation.

We had just about topped the rise when I saw the fawn. The animal was lying next to a small sagebrush bush facing our direction and we were spotted immediately.

My eyes had barely made contact with the little deer when it jumped from its bed and dashed away. Instantly it was joined by other deer, and the herd ran out of sight. I never saw the buck, but I was sure he was present.

Judi and I ran to the top of the knoll, and I told her to get ready. It was possible the deer would show themselves as they scrambled away in the open country.

Suddenly the animals appeared about 175 yards away. They walked nervously, looking around for the source of danger. Only the fawn had seen us; the rest fled spontaneously.

Judi was in a sitting position, the rifle trained on the walking buck.

"Should I wait for him to stop?" she asked.

"No," I whispered. "He's walking slowly. Aim for the front part of his chest and squeeze the trigger."

"I'm too nervous, Dad," she said. "I can't hold the gun steady."

I saw the muzzle wavering slightly, and knew that Judi was having trouble. At that moment she fired, and I saw the bullet kick up dust over the buck's back.

The deer took three long bounds and disappeared over a ridge. He was gone.

Judi didn't say a word, but I could see tears welling in her eyes.

"C'mon kid," I said, "let's go find another one. There are plenty more deer out here."

We trudged along, walking in the general direction that the spooked deer took.

Fifteen minutes later, when topping a crest, we were surprised by a clatter of rocks below us. We had blundered into the same herd of deer.

Judi needed no instructions. She quickly laid prone on the ridge, drew a bead on the buck, and killed him instantly. In just a few seconds, she became a hunter. Years of practice and dreaming were finally rewarded.

Needless to say, I was a mighty proud and happy Dad at that moment in time.

I walk softly through powder snow, trying to spot a bedded buck at the edge of the timber.

PLEASE, PLEASE, SHOOT THAT BUCK!

It's no secret that the Grey's River area in western Wyoming is one of my all-time favorite muley hunting spots. A number of years ago, I hunted the region with my pal, Gabby Barrus, who lives in Cody, Wyoming. At the time I was a Utah resident. I didn't know it then, of course, but one day I too would be a resident of Cody. I had Gabby to thank for that decision, because I frequently drove to Cody to pick him up on the way to Yellowstone Park where we'd photograph wildlife. Through Gabby, I discovered Cody and fell in love with the town and surrounding area.

This particular hunt was with Grant Barrus, who was not related to Gabby. I had a tag for only one region in Grey's River, because as a nonresident I was entitled to hunt only the region I'd drawn. Gabby was a resident and could hunt the entire state. (This was just one reason why I decided Wyoming was being unfair to nonresident hunters. To get even, I'd move to the state. And I did. And I love it here......)

At one point in the hunt, we were riding horseback high up in the Bridger-Teton Forest. On that particular day, we'd crossed into a region

Grant Barrus points out a good spot to Gabby high up in the Wyoming Range.

I couldn't hunt in. I brought my cameras along to take photos.

As we neared the top of a ridge above a spectacular basin, the guide whispered to get ready. According to him, there was ALWAYS a big buck in the basin.

He was right. We were walking our horses down into the basin when a huge buck bounded out. Gabby and the other hunters scrambled for their guns, but it was too late. Within seconds, the buck was swallowed up in the timber.

Later in the day, we were riding along the trail, when an absolutely monster buck sprang up out of a small blowdown next to the trail. I was riding the last horse; another hunter was in front of me, and Grant was several yards in front of him. Gabby, another hunter and a guide were hunting somewhere else.

When the giant buck hit the top of the ridge 70 yards away, it stopped to look at us. I told the hunter to quickly get off his horse, and he did. I flew off my horse, pulled it off the trail, and ran around to grab the reins of the hunter's horse so he'd be rid of the animal.

The hunter stood there, aiming at the big buck, and hesitated. Unbelievably, the buck stood still.

Hunters ride through big buck country in Wyoming's Grey's River area.

"Shoot!" I said.

The hunter stood there quietly, still aiming at the buck.

"Good Lord, shoot!" I said again.

Still no shot.

"What's WRONG!" I stated. "Why don't you shoot?"

Finally the hunter answered. "That's no deer," he said, "that's a bull elk!"

You could have gotten the same reaction from me by hitting me over the head with a sledgehammer. I was dumbfounded.

"It's a buck!" I stammered, "the biggest buck you'll see in a lifetime."

Still no shot. The man didn't believe me. This was his first western hunt; he'd never seen a muley before. Perhaps he had no perception of what a super buck looked like. This was absolutely a super buck. Obviously he didn't know what a bull elk looked like, either.

Predictably, the monster buck took a leap over the rim and disappeared. I felt as helpless and frustrated as I ever had in a lifetime of hunting. Because we weren't in my region, my tag was no good for that spot.

Suddenly Grant appeared, riding briskly toward us.

"Didn't you see that buck?" he said to the hunter. "That one was a dandy. There aren't many like that in the entire state of Wyoming."

The hunter didn't say anything, and Grant didn't press the issue. Perhaps he saw the look of anguish on the hunter's face. I didn't say anything, either. Nothing was said about the buck over dinner that night, no doubt to the hunter's great relief.

I saw another huge buck on that trip, but it wasn't in the cards for him to wear my tag. Gabby and I were riding together when two enormous bucks appeared in the fog as far as you could see, which was about 600 yards away. We immediately dismounted to try a sneak, but the fog wafted in, obscuring the bucks. When it finally drifted away, the deer were gone. We never saw them again.

That hunt was one of the first occasions when I said to heck with being a Wyoming nonresident. It started the ball rolling. I picked up the ball, kept it in the correct court, and finally made the move. I've never been happier.

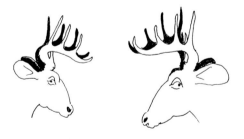

EDITORS ARE HUMAN, TOO

A curious thing happens to me practically every fall. Because I live in the West and most outdoor magazines are published on the East Coast, I often host eastern editors and writers on big game hunts. These are all pals, and the hunts are almost always memorable occasions. Guiding my friends is fun; never a chore.

Because I was raised in the East and vividly remember my impressions of the West when I first moved there, I know exactly how my friends feel when they're treated to a Rocky Mountain hunt.

When they look at the awesome Rockies and say, "My God, what a magnificent place," I know where they're coming from. And when they down their first mule deer, antelope, or elk, I also know precisely what they're feeling. To me, it's a joy to share their tremendous satisfaction at just seeing the Rockies, as well as their reactions when they take their first western big game animal.

Of course, plenty of humorous situations have occurred during those hunts, some of which I'll elaborate on in this chapter, but I'll use fictitious names to protect both the innocent and guilty parties.

One year, I drew a buffalo tag in Utah. This was a big deal, sort of like hitting a major cash lottery. The buffalo herd was truly wild, roaming the rugged Henry Mountains. I was beside myself with joy when I learned I'd drawn a tag, but I'd committed myself to guiding a writer pal from the east long before I learned I'd drawn a buffalo tag. I'll call my friend Sidney.

Our schedule included a pheasant hunt in South Dakota, and then a muley hunt in Colorado near the Utah border. When I drew the buffalo tag, however, I sandwiched the first two days of the season between the bird and deer hunts. Sidney would go along with me on the buffalo hunt. If I didn't score, I'd return after Sidney went home.

As it turned out, I didn't get a buffalo those first two days, but I scored later on in the season. I won't tell you about that wild and wacky buffalo hunt now; you'll have to read about it in my forthcoming book, *TO HECK WITH BIG GAME HUNTING.*

Sidney and I hunted for deer in Colorado in an area that was always rewarding for me. Unfortunately, we had bad luck the first couple days, and had only one day to go when I tried a new spot.

I put Sidney on stand and walked through an oak brush thicket that usually sheltered a big old mossyhorn buck. Small drives are among my favorite techniques, and this one worked perfectly.

A huge buck erupted from cover, and bounded across a sagebrush slope. As luck would have it, really bad luck, the deer ran straight east, into a glaring, early morning sun. My buddy was blinded by the sun and couldn't see the buck in his scope. The deer got away unscathed, and my pal never saw another buck that day. At least he went home with a bunch of fat rooster pheasants from our South Dakota hunt.

Another time I put another writer friend on stand. I'll call him Sam. We were hunting a pretty mountainside with quaking aspens in the draws and patches of oak brush on the sidehills.

I positioned Sam in a small basin where he had an unobstructed view of the area around him. Making a circle around the rimrock, I flushed a dandy buck, a real beauty, and it headed precisely for Sam, who I couldn't see at the time.

I waited for a shot, but it never came. I couldn't imagine what was going on, because Sam should have easily seen the brute of a buck.

When I got to a point where I could see Sam, I immediately learned why he hadn't shot — it's pretty tough to shoot when you're looking at the insides of your eyelids. Sam was fast asleep; I could hear him snoring 100 yards away.

Sam deserved to be punished. I aimed my .30/06 at a safe backdrop and fired a round. Sam jumped about 10 feet in the air, or so it seemed, and came up sputtering and mumbling. I chastised him thoroughly about his untimely nap, but Sam defended himself by saying that the high altitude had made him just a touch sleepy. That nap cost him a superb buck.

The next day Sam had to catch a plane in midafternoon. We had the morning to hunt, and I planned a drive in another area. I left Sam in a good spot and climbed high above him.

When I got to a lofty peak, I looked down and saw that my truck headlights were on. I cussed myself, because if the battery wore down and the truck wouldn't start, Sam would surely miss his flight. He had an important appointment the next day.

I hurried through the aspens and jumped a bunch of deer. One was a very nice four-point buck, and he was headed for Sam. There were a couple places where the buck could get around Sam unseen; I hoped the muley wouldn't take one of those routes.

He did. Sam never saw the buck, and the hunt was over. We hurried down to the truck, and it started nicely. Sam made his plane, and planned another hunt with me the following year.

That hunt went much better. Sam got a deer, a decent buck with four points to the side, but I never let him forget about the beauty that he never saw because of his nap.

Another time, a bunch of pals from Pennsylvania hunted with me in Wyoming. Given the fact that I was longing for some good imported Italian cold cuts and cheese, they brought out a wonderful supply of goodies. It's tough to find the real thing in small Rocky Mountain towns that I frequented.

During lunch break one afternoon, my friends spread out a marvelous lunch on the tailgate of my pickup. I was making my way to the truck, wandering through a bunch of junipers along the highway, when unbeknown to me, I kicked out a small buck. It ran across the highway where it was spotted by the boys setting up the tailgate party. One of the men grabbed his rifle, ran off into the timber where the buck disappeared, and shot it.

I heard the shot and ran across the road toward where the other men were pointing. I entered the trees and saw my pal aiming straight down below his position, as if he were aiming at one of his toes. Suddenly he fired and I thought they were playing a joke on me.

It was no joke. My friend hit the buck, but it required another shot. The hunter finished it off as the buck stood near the base of the cliff beneath him.

The tailgate party was great. To top it off, each of the other hunters got their bucks that afternoon,

A hunt in snowy mountain country almost resulted in a writer friend getting a huge muley, but it didn't quite work out that way. I arrived late in the hunt, and my pal, who I'll call Willy, was guided by a veteran outdoorsman, the kind of character who didn't have much to say about anything. When he spoke, however, you listened, because it was generally a profound statement. This guide was also a laid back gentleman who seldom got much excited about anything.

He and Willy were riding across a snowy slope, when a big buck appeared. The guide pointed it out to the hunter, who immediately dismounted.

"Is he a good buck?" Willy asked. I should point out that this was Willy's first mule deer hunt. He had no idea what to expect in the way of antler size.

"Yep, he's a good buck," the guide responded simply.

"How good?" Willy asked.

"Good buck," the guide drawled.

"Is he better than average?" questioned the hunter.

"Shoot the buck," the guide said.

During this short conversation, the buck was getting more and more fidgety. He wasn't about to stand and stare at the men much longer. Willy found a good rest, as the buck was about 200 yards away, and by the time he was ready to shoot, the buck disappeared. There was no shot, and the guide said nothing much, other than it was getting late and they ought to be heading back to camp.

I arrived that evening and heard Willy's story. Later I saw the guide alone, and asked him how big the buck was.

The guide tipped his hat back, thought about my question a moment, and came forth with an answer.

"Biggest damned buck I ever seen in these parts," he said. At that he shrugged, pulled out a can of Copenhagen, stuffed a wad under his lip, and shuffled off to the horse corral.

A hunt with an *OUTDOOR LIFE* editor turned out exceptionally well. I'll call him by his real name, Ralph Stuart, because Ralph can be proud of the hunt.

He and I were hunting on a ranch in New Mexico leased by U.S. Outfitters, a company out of Taos. Elk were our chief quarry, though a few good bucks were known to live in the area.

Ralph got a very nice bull, and turned his attention to muleys. I'd been telling him that big old muley bucks were just as smart as whitetails, and not to expect much.

With those words ringing in his ears, he set off with one of the guides, while I went elsewhere to look for a bull elk.

That evening, Ralph and his guide were all smiles. He'd killed a beautiful buck, one of the loveliest typical four-points I'd ever laid eyes on. As they told the story, they were making their way along a fence line when they spotted the buck, it's nose in the ground as it nibbled on a bush.

Ralph simply drew a bead on the buck and shot him where he stood. So much for the challenge and difficulty of hunting great big bucks. At that point I figured my hunting strategies were all wrong. Maybe I should start walking more fence lines.

Another hunt with an eastern editor turned out to have a happy ending as well. Bill Rooney, a former *OUTDOOR LIFE* editor and currently editor of *AMERICAN FORESTS* magazine, hunted with me in Utah.

On opening weekend we headed for the mountains before shooting light and I turned Bill out in a good area while I continued on to hunt elsewhere. With sunrise came plenty of shooting from every direction.

I was disgusted with the crowds of hunters around us, and headed back to find Bill. We weren't supposed to meet until noon; maybe I could follow his tracks in the snow and catch up and we could hunt another area I knew.

Bill was easy to find. He was sitting along the highway, eating a sandwich, next to a buck he'd killed, field dressed, and dragged to the road. He was happy as a clam, completely satisfied with the buck he'd taken. Those are the kinds of hunts, and hunters, I like. Bill was raised in the east, and every time he hunts with me he constantly marvels at the beauty of the Rockies. Getting an animal was the frosting on the cake. If he didn't get a critter and there was no frosting, the cake was just as

Editor Ralph Stuart with a magnificent muley he took in New Mexico.

delicious.

One particular acquaintance who hunted with me had never seen a muley in the flesh prior to his western hunt. At one point he passed on a modest four-point buck while we hunted in deep snow.

I told him if he didn't want the buck, I'd take it. My back was giving me trouble at the time, and I wasn't in much of a mood to fight deep snow.

When I killed the buck and we walked up to it, my friend took a look and shook his head, staring at the buck's 25-inch wide rack.

"That's a pretty good buck," he said, "but I had no idea that four-pointers could be so small. I thought they were all monsters, with 30-inch racks."

My companion had been reading too many magazines that showed massive muleys. He had no idea what to expect and ultimately went home with an unfilled tag. I suspect he said to heck with passing up fair bucks on future hunts. I don't blame him.

As time goes on, I'll continue to take my editor pals hunting. If nothing more, they get a sense of reality when they hunt the western woods. That reality is infused into their judgement when they make magazine decisions, which in turn improves the quality of the magazine.

Don't expect them to always tell the exact and honest truth about their hunting trips, though. I know better.

They told me I shot the ranch mascot. He made darned good jerky, though.

I SHOT THE RANCH MASCOT

MY GAD YOU SHOT BAMBI!

It was one of those frustrating hunts when nothing seemed to work out right. I was after elk in Montana's Centennial Valley, based out of Keith Rush's ranch. Keith runs a full-time outfitting service out of his place, taking fishermen in the summer, and hunters in the fall. He also offers an excellent guide school in the summer.

Keith and I have been pals for years. I love to hunt in his area, because it's a beautiful part of the world and also has plenty of game. We have a relationship where I can come through unannounced in the middle of the night, find an empty cot in one of the numerous cabins, and have a hot breakfast in the morning. Many times I'll hunt on my own, basing out of the ranch.

This is especially fun in late November, when heavy snow covers the mountains. Elk drop down low, and muleys are in the rut. It's a perfect combination for both species.

On this particular hunt, I couldn't get up close to a bull elk, no matter how hard I tried. Conditions were perfect for tracking in the snow, but bulls remained elusive in the timber. Muleys were hard to find, too. There are some around in Keith's area, but not as many as in other spots. He's basically in elk country.

Things looked bleak when the last day arrived. It was my last hunt of the year, and I'd hoped to bring some meat home for my annual jerky supply. Each fall I make up a big batch of jerky to last a full year. A couple quarters of elk or a deer would be just the ticket. My kids devour my homemade jerky, as I do and most other people who try it. I'd already taken an elk that fall in Wyoming, but it was already processed into steaks, burger, roasts, and my homemade sausage. Another critter would have been perfect for jerky.

At breakfast the last morning, I chatted with Kevin Rush, Keith's son, who is a fine guide and a fun guy to be around. I told Keith I was looking for a jerky buck, and he suggested I try behind the horse corral. He'd seen a small buck and a bunch of does hanging around in the timber. Since the rut was on, the buck would no doubt stay with the does.

I'd given up on elk, because I had to leave that evening. It would have taken an extra day to get a carcass out if I got an elk in the afternoon. Besides, I'd already killed a bull, and I didn't really need another for my jerky supply. A deer would be just right.

I headed for the horse corral, and still hunted quietly through the trees. Deer tracks were everywhere, and there was a fresh moose track as well. Sooner or later I'd find the deer, and I was confident the buck would be with them.

A half hour later, I spotted a doe nibbling on a bush. She was about 20 yards away and hadn't detected me because the wind was just right, and the snow was soft and dry, offering quiet walking.

I froze in my tracks and raised my rifle. I knew the buck was close, and I spotted him almost instantly. He was bedded about 10 yards from the doe, along with two other does, also bedded.

I centered him in my scope and fired. The hunt was over; I had my annual supply of jerky meat.

The buck was about 35 yards out, offering a perfect neck shot. He was a small three-pointer, just about what I was looking for.

I dragged the buck several hundred yards through the snow to a point where I could drive to him. Then I walked back to the ranch to pack up my gear. I ran into Kevin and thanked him for the tip about the buck.

"You didn't really shoot that little buck, did you?" he said.

"Why?", I asked, "wasn't I supposed to?"

"Hell, that was the ranch mascot," Kevin replied. "The kids fed him every day. He'd been around since he was a fawn. I was just kidding when I told you to shoot him. I thought you knew I was joking around."

"Geez," I said. "I had no idea. I thought it was okay to hunt for him."

"What the hell will I tell the kids," Kevin said. "Man, they're going to be upset. I hate it when kids cry a lot and make a big fuss."

By now I was feeling like the world's biggest jerk. I shot the pet deer; Bambi was dead. The kids will hate me, and I'll never be welcome on the ranch again.

I was suddenly terribly depressed, feeling like a snake in the grass. I walked over to my bunkhouse to finish packing, wanting to be out of there with the buck before the kids saw it. I didn't want to face the music.

Quickly packing, I threw my gear in my truck and went over to say goodbye to whoever was in the ranch mess hall. I hoped I didn't run into any kids.

Kevin was drinking a cup of coffee when I entered. I immediately began apologizing for shooting the tame deer when Kevin broke out laughing.

"What are you laughing about," I said. "It's not funny."

"Sure it is, "Kevin said. "The funny part is that you believed me. That buck just showed up a couple days ago, just like they do every year. When the rut is on, a buck will trail in here and hang out with the does in the horse pasture."

I was enormously relieved, and called Kevin some unprintable names. The joke was on me, but I smiled every time I had a piece of jerky for a snack. Mascot or not, it was a fine eating little buck.

I show off this nice high-racked buck. He's no trophy class animal, but a good representative buck muley.

WHEN SINGING PAYS OFF

It was about 1980 when I was invited to hunt mule deer on the Deseret Ranch in northern Utah. This particular piece of property is enormous; I believe it covers some 400,000 acres.

For many years the ranch was owned by a number of stockmen who grazed it extensively. As I recall, hunting was essentially unrestricted, costing about $10 for season access. You paid as you entered one of the ranch gates. Trouble is, several thousand hunters from nearby Salt Lake City and Ogden hunted the place to death. The average bucks were small because of the consistent harvest, though a few brutes managed to escape every year.

The ranchers decided to sell the property and offered a deal to the Utah Division of Wildlife Resources. The amount of money needed to buy it was considerable, and state law required a public vote in a referendum.

I don't know who caused the deal to fall through; many people believe the Division of Wildlife Resources didn't have an effective PR program. Whatever the case, Utah voters decided to spend the money on some improvements at the state fairgrounds rather than on an incredibly gorgeous chunk of real estate that would have been the property of the state with hunting rights available to the citizens. It was a shame. Many state employees, including game warden pals, tried hard to get the word out, but the land deal failed regardless.

An oriental gentleman from Hong Kong bought the ranch and public hunting immediately ceased, as predicted. A ranch and wildlife manager were hired to come up with a management plan for livestock and wildlife.

As a first step, the managers drastically curtailed hunting pressure which, in my opinion, was a good move. The herd needed a break from the intensive harvests to give bucks a few years of protection in order to grow decent antlers.

I was invited to hunt the ranch with the express purpose of writing a story about it and attracting some attention to its potential of producing good bucks. At that point in time, a very reasonable fee was charged, which allowed you to trespass, hunt, and camp on the ranch for the entire 11-day season. A quota of about 200 tags were offered.

Knowing a good thing when I see it, I quickly accepted the invitation, and was eager to hunt the property. Its ability to produce big bucks was well-known around the state as well as in trophy deer hunting circles.

My hunt was short and sweet. I went out with the ranch manager, and looked over a number of dandy bucks, but I passed, hoping to see the buck of a lifetime.

Just before dark, we saw a big buck feeding on a slope. We stalked in close, and got within 50 yards by moving in behind him by making a big circle. As soon as I saw the buck he spotted me as well, and he took off down the mountain.

There's an interesting illusion regarding antlered animals that are running directly away from you. A decent-racked animal will often look twice its size; at least, to me they do.

This buck looked like a giant, and the ranch manager agreed that it was an excellent deer. I shot it as it lumbered up the opposite slope, dropping it instantly with a bullet placed in the base of its neck.

Closer inspection revealed it wasn't quite as big as it looked, but I was nonetheless happy. It was a very nice buck.

I wrote an article about the ranch, and the response from readers was quite enthusiastic. In fact, the reaction was so enormous that ranch personnel didn't have to advertise. More than 1,500 inquiries were received as a result of my story.

Because the ranch people were pleased, they invited me back for another hunt the following year as a gesture of thanks. Again I accepted, and again I was looking forward to my biggest buck ever.

This time I hunted on my own, and towed my camp trailer. Officials requested that I park next to the main gate, which was fine, but I was constantly visited by other hunters who wanted to see what I'd killed. Because I wrote a book on mule deer, everyone figured I was superman in the deer woods. They expected me to shoot the biggest deer on the ranch.

I wish it worked that way, but it doesn't. I hunt hard, but I'm never guaranteed a trophy-class animal just because I wrote a book on the subject.

The first day I hunted out of the high camp, which was probably 9,500 feet or so. The temperature turned cold, and heavy snow hindered access, so I stayed in a small bunkhouse by myself rather than fighting snow drifts to get back to my camper.

Since my sleeping bag was in the camper, I borrowed an extra bag from one of the ranch hands. It was a lightweight summer model, and was useless in the little frigid cabin.

I tried building a fire in the woodstove, but I couldn't get one going. That was a memorable event, because I'm pretty proud of my fire-starting abilities. That was one of the only times I can remember that I couldn't get a fire to take. The wood in the cabin was green, and I broke the blade of one of my favorite pocket knives by trying to split small slivers as kindling.

It was a long, cold night, and I was in my truck long before sunrise, heading for a hunting area and reveling in the warmth of the heater.

I still hunted through snowy woods and saw several bucks, but nothing I wanted to shoot. Later, while driving to lower elevations, a good buck dashed across the road in front of me. At any other time I would have scrambled out, but for some reason I decided to let him go. As soon as he disappeared, I was mad at myself, but I soon got over it. I didn't want to shoot a deer from alongside a vehicle, at least, not on the Deseret Ranch.

That afternoon I walked a series of small ridges. The draws between them were choked with quaking aspens, while the ridgetops and upper slopes were covered with sagebrush. It was a perfect place to jump deer.

At one spot I tossed rocks into the aspens below me. Almost instantly a bunch of deer exploded from the cover and bounded up the opposite open slope. At least three bucks were in the herd, but none were what I was looking for.

Everything quieted down in the brush, and I had a strange hunch that all the deer hadn't left. I had a silly notion to start singing at the top of my voice to spook any lingering animals.

I sang, and nothing happened. Then I sang some more, keeping it up for 10 minutes. I was enjoying myself immensely.

After a few minutes of such nonsense, I was surprised to see a big buck crash out of the trees. Indeed, he had opted to hide rather than to run, and he didn't run out the way the other deer did. Instead, he stayed in the trees, offering me a poor shot. The buck would have been most welcome, but I never tried a shot at him in the brush. He got away unscathed.

That night, several hunters visited me in my camper by the gate. I had no good news for them, but we shared plenty of tales. Being parked at the gate offered me the opportunity of seeing all the deer taken each day, since hunters had to check their animals with the biologist who worked the gate. A number of excellent muleys had been taken, and I knew it was only a matter of time before I got mine.

The next day, I worked my way into a beautiful basin ringed by aspen trees. Sitting quietly on a log, I heard a crashing sound below me. Suddenly a lovely buck appeared, running for all he was worth. All I had was a profile view, but his antlers seemed tall with good forks.

He looked plenty good. I shouldered my .30/06 and held just a touch in front of his shoulder. The muley collapsed on the spot when the bullet hit him squarely in the shoulder.

I was mighty pleased with the buck. He was a handsome animal, not even close to record book quality, but a pretty four-point. His outside spread was right at 28 inches.

After field dressing him, I dragged the deer down the mountain slope to a road. I was delighted that it was a downhill drag, because I estimated his dressed weight at around 195 pounds.

I was attempting to load the buck in my truck alone and was having a tough time of it when a bunch of hunters pulled up. I recognized one as being a dedicated trophy hunter, and when he saw my buck he had a funny look on his face.

"I didn't think YOU would kill a small buck like that," he said. "I figured you'd hold out for a real buster."

I was taken aback by his comment. I was perfectly satisfied with my deer, and wasn't about to be intimidated by some character who didn't think it was worthy.

I didn't have much of an answer for the guy. Hunting means more to me than getting a trophy, but I didn't think he'd understand. I don't have much patience with people who judge their hunt by the size of the animal they go home with.

To heck with trophy hunting. Give me the magnificence of mule deer country, of the sweet air, the mountains to climb, and the sights to be seen. That's what it's all about.

Vin Sparano, Editor-in-chief of OUTDOOR LIFE magazine, with a fine muley he took in Wyoming. He and I took two bucks on camera while doing my mule deer hunting video.

SHOWTIME IN THE DEER WOODS

I've always figured that hunting is meant to be a personal activity, certainly not a spectator sport. The sudden interest in hunting videos, however, has made hunting exactly that. Hunters and the quarry appear regularly in hundreds of video productions, and can be viewed by anyone who cares to watch.

I've done four hunting videos, two on elk, one on bighorn sheep, and one on mule deer. The latter was a most interesting time of my life, taking about 28 days to complete.

The video was produced by 3M corporation, under the very capable direction of Jerry Chiappetta, a Michigan outdoor personality who is one of the best in the business. Jerry, his wife, Rita, two technicians and I lived much of that time in Saratoga, Wyoming, where most of the video was filmed.

The mule deer video was the last of the four I'd done. I figured I was a veteran in show business before I met Jerry, but he taught me a great deal about being on-camera.

For one thing, he taught me how to relax and to smile. That might not seem to be a big deal, but I can assure you, when the camera is pointed at your face and you have certain lines to say, and those lines must be said flawlessly and with certain inflections, it IS a big deal. Ask anyone who is experienced in the motion picture business.

Before we even began shooting, we had to have a script. 3M hired a writer to come up with a script, with much of the information coming from my hardcover book, *HUNTING AMERICA'S MULE DEER.* To make sure the writer was in synch with what we were doing, he flew out to Wyoming, and I showed him around mule deer country for a week. Then I had to fly to 3M's headquarters in Minnesota to hammer out details for the video.

Jerry and the 3M people were thorough in their preparation for the film. When the crew arrived in Wyoming, everything was pretty cut and dried — except cooperation from mule deer. The script called for a kill on film — a clean kill. The buck had to be humanely dispatched. In other words, he had to drop to the ground at the shot and not wiggle. This was a tough task, because practically every perfectly hit heart and lung-shot animal will run some distance before falling over. I was most definitely worried about the kill shot.

The weather cooperated nicely. Balmy fall days allowed for good camera work, with the least amount of complications for the technical equipment. Rain, snow, and cold temperatures would have caused all sorts of problems.

A slight problem was caused by the requirement of me reading my lines from cue cards. Ideally, I memorized the lines, and got through the sequence with a minimum of takes. A "take" is a single filming session. When the take was finally as near to perfect as possible, it was called a "wrap". When I was lucky, we could get a wrap with as few as two takes. We never got through a scene with a single take, because Jerry always wanted an extra one for insurance. Some hidden gremlin or glitch could have crept in and messed up an otherwise good take. When that was the case, we had another to fall back on.

Sometimes, because of technical difficulties, external noises such as airplanes and vehicles, and my screwing up the dialogue, it took as many as a dozen takes. Those were times calling for the utmost of patience, fortitude, and a hell of a sense of humor.

The problem with my reading the cards was my lousy eyesight. I've worn glasses since I was 14, and Jerry wanted me on camera without glasses. On many occasions I couldn't read the doggoned cue card, which was held up next to the camera by a technician. If the camera was too close, you could see my eyes move as I read the words. That was a no-no. So I ended up memorizing the cue cards.

Quite often Jerry liked me to read the card off-camera, get a grasp of its message, and do the take in my own words. This was often the way it happened, but even a tiny stumble on a one syllable word required another damnable take.

All sorts of minor problems interfered with our shooting. I'd do a perfect take, and was pleased as punch, when the technician would say, "did you hear that airplane going over? I think it screwed up the take." Sure enough, we'd reshoot the scene.

Another fun irritation was a technical problem. Just as I was rolling along with a smooth dialogue, the technician would shout "Cut", because he ran out of tape, there was a problem with the sound, the camera wasn't focused correctly, or one of a thousand other little problems that could drive you insane.

It was one thing to be set up in a nice scene where the set was controlled by lights, everyone was composed, and the scene was tidy. It was quite another thing to do the actual kill scene. In that case, nothing was controlled. We were victims of that particular area, the current weather conditions, the actions of the buck, terrain, and a myriad of other factors. Murphy's Law seemed to be constantly lurking.

Most of the instructional part of the video was done before deer season. I described hunt strategies, mule deer behavior patterns, variations in mule deer country, preferred forage species, and other pertinent background information.

As all this was going on, I was anxious for opening day to arrive so we could get the project over with. After 20 some days of this non-stop movie work, I was ready to get on with my life and live like a real human being. Show business was becoming a major headache.

To photograph the kill, everything had to be right. The deer had to be very visible and in focus, I had to be in the foreground of the scene with the buck out in front of me, and the shot had to be perfect. The muley had to drop instantly, and all the technical equipment had to be working properly.

It was a tall order, but we got the job done. The first opportunity was on a slope where I'd spotted six dandy bucks just at daybreak. We crept close with our burgeoning gear and four-man crew, and we got everything nicely lined up.

The bucks finally spotted us, and I picked the best of the bunch, trying to communicate to the cameraman which one I was going to shoot. I was ready to squeeze the trigger, waiting for Jerry's signal, but instead I heard "CUT". Something had happened to the equipment, the buck got away, and we had no kill.

Practically the same thing happened a day later. Once again I was ready to knock down a big buck, but was stopped by one of the crew because of a technical problem.

My boss, Vin Sparano, who was Executive Editor of *OUTDOOR LIFE* (and is now Editor-in-Chief), came out to hunt with me before the kill shot was concluded. Vin joined us, and the following morning we spotted a nice buck on a mountain. After making a big circle afoot, with the camera crew trailing, we jumped the buck, but he ran off in the wrong direction. The camera crew wasn't ready.

The next day we spotted five nice bucks in a bunch. We dropped out of sight and made a careful stalk. Vin was with me; by some miracle we might get TWO kills on film.

As we topped a knoll, I saw the bucks just 70 yards away feeding in the bottom of a shallow draw. I nodded back at the cameraman, told him to get ready, and I positioned myself for the shot.

I inched up, centered the buck in my scope, and heard wonderful news from the crew. It was a simple series of words that went: "shoot when you're ready."

I was ready, and I shot. The buck dropped hard to the ground, and the other four bucks took off. Vin shot, his buck fell hard to the ground, and I couldn't believe our good luck. Then I realized that something just HAD to be wrong with the equipment, or our positioning, or something else.

My fears were unfounded. It was a perfect take. Two dead bucks, and two damned happy hunters, especially me. A couple more days of shooting horseback scenes concluded the video, and Vin and I went on to hunt antelope elsewhere.

It's fun to watch the video, but that's the end of the fun. The rest is hard work. I can definitely say to heck with hunting on camera forever more. Unless, of course, they want me to do a hunt with Farah, or someone of equal pulchritudinal assets.

Which reminds me, I once hunted Dall sheep in Alaska with a lass who was a former Dallas Cowboys cheerleader. Watch for that story in my upcoming book, *TO HECK WITH BIG GAME HUNTING.*

Boots R. Reynolds

A lot has been said about Boots Reynolds, but most of it can't be printed. One printable comment was made, however, by a friend, who said, "He can buck a fella off harder with a paintbrush than any bronc I've ever seen!" Maybe that's because Boots has been down lookin' up enough times himself.

Boots is really Roy Reynolds, who was born and raised on the ranches of the Osage country of Oklahoma. It was on these ranches that he got his education as a cowboy. He's been on, over, under and around horses all his life and his career began at the age of eight as a brush track jockey riding matched races in Oklahoma.

Somehow in the early 70's Boots ended up in northern Idaho where he now resides with his wife, Becky, overlooking beautiful Lake Pend Oreille near Sandpoint, Idaho, and where he devotes himself full-time to drawing and painting.

Always seeing humor in his surroundings, it was just a matter of time until his drawings became cartoons. After years of drawing these "funny pitchers" for friends and family he decided to try his hand at sharing them with the public. Somebody, somewhere, must have liked them as his pen and ink cartoons have appeared in such magazines as *Western Horseman, Horseman, Prorodeo Sports News, Horse and Horseman,* and *Horse and Rider.*

Somehow, despite the demand and popularity of his artwork, Boots has managed to find some spare pieces to hang in a few galleries. (Rumor has it that he pays them to hang his paintings.) He now has his work displayed in galleries in Issaquah, Washington; Coeur d'Alene, Idaho; and Cody, Wyoming.

According to Boots, "I think the western art world and the public are ready for something a little different and the way things are going in the world we could all use a little more humor and I plan to give it to them. They can laugh at my stuff all they want to."

To order a print of the book cover and other humorous prints by Boots write for information and brochure to: R. Place, 195 Trestle Creek Rd., Hope, Idaho, 83836.

Books and Videos
by
Jim Zumbo

BOOKS

All books will be autographed

TO HECK WITH ELK HUNTING — Jim's favorite hunting tales. Most are humorous, but some are bizarre. Illustrated by Boots Reynolds. $20.95 postpaid.

TO HECK WITH DEER HUNTING — Jim takes a look, often humorous, at deer hunting episodes across the country throughout his long hunting career. Illustrated by Boots Reynolds. $20.95 postpaid.

CALLING ALL ELK — The only book on the subject of elk hunting that covers every aspect of elk vocalization. $17.95 postpaid.

HUNT ELK — The most comprehensive book ever written on elk hunting. This 260-page hardcover describes everything you've ever wanted to know about elk — bugling, hunting in timber, late season hunting, trophy hunting, solid advice on hunting on your own or with an outfitter, and lots more. $27.95 postpaid.

HUNTING AMERICA'S MULE DEER — The first book ever done on every phase of mule deer hunting. This thick 360-page hardcover is acclaimed to be the best on the subject. Plenty of photos, with valuable information on trophy hunting and where-to, and how-to hunt muley bucks. $22.95 postpaid.

HOW TO PLAN YOUR WESTERN BIG GAME HUNT — Are you dreaming of a western hunt? This softcover will start you in the right direction, with solid info on planning your hunt. Lots of maps and phone numbers, and precise info on all western big game species. $11.95 postpaid.

VIDEOS

HUNTING BUGLING ELK WITH JIM ZUMBO — Produced by Sportsmen On Film — 70 minutes. Watch Jim fly in to Idaho's Selway wilderness and hunt elk. This video is loaded with instructions and tips on elk bugling, and is climaxed by Jim taking a big 6-point bull on camera. $29.95 postpaid.

LATE SEASON ELK WITH JIM ZUMBO — Produced by Sportsmen on Film — 38 minutes. See huge elk plowing through deep powder snow, and watch a 12-year old boy take a big bull on camera. Lots of tips and techniques included. $29.95 postpaid.

HUNTING AMERICA'S MULE DEER — Produced by 3M Corp. — 60 minutes. Acclaimed to be the best mule deer video ever produced. Watch Jim stalk and kill a nice four-point buck. Plenty of specific info on techniques. Filmed in Wyoming. $29.95 postpaid.

HUNTING BIGHORN SHEEP WITH JIM ZUMBO — Produced by Grunkmeyer Productions — 60 minutes. Watch Jim stalk and shoot a ram in Wyoming's spectacular Teton Wilderness with veteran outfitter Nate Vance. $52.95 postpaid.

AUDIO CASSETTES

E-Z CALL INSTRUCTIONAL TAPE — 30 minutes. Jim Zumbo tells where, how and when to use the E-Z Elk Call, including hunt scenarios and situations. $12.95 postpaid.

E-Z ELK CALL

JIM ZUMBO'S COW CALL — Made of very soft plastic, both calling edges are of different lengths, allow calls of varying pitches. $12.95 postpaid.

Order from:

JIM ZUMBO
P.O. Box 2390
Cody, Wyoming 82414

Check, money order or Visa/MC accepted. Credit card orders: please include number and expiration date. Allow 6 weeks for delivery. Canadian residents add $2.00 for each item for shipping.